French Cars from 1920 to 1925

French Cars
from 1920 to 1925

Pierre Dumont

Translated by John V. Bolster

FREDERICK WARNE

ISBN 0 7232 2116 2

Filmset and printed in Great Britain by BAS Printers Limited, Over
Wallop, Hampshire

Contents

Acknowledgements

A certain number of documents illustrating this book are reproduced from publications of the period (*La Vie Automobile* and *L'Auto Catalogue*). The photos taken specially are by Pierre Autef, and the author wishes to thank those who have helped him to complete his documentation: Serge Pozzoli, Benoît Pèrot and Michael Clapham as well as the archives of Citroën, Peugeot, and Renault.

Introduction

There must have been round about a thousand French industrialists, mechanics, or experimenters, who have tried since the turn of the century, with more or less good fortune, to manufacture cars. Of these, probably three hundred firms were active between 1920 and 1925.

Some have left just a name, a make that one quotes without knowing any details, while others disappeared after a single motor show or public presentation; only a few found glory in competition or achieved commercial success. Whether their output rose to mass production or was limited to three or four cars, whether they were known for their sensible and orthodox designs or, on the contrary, for the originality of their ideas, all, without exception, have the right to the title *manufacturer*. Quite a number of the smaller producers may now be considered the best, for their technical qualities or the performances they achieved, without regard to their production figures.

An author might have all the necessary material, the works of reference, and the knowledge, to write about those thousand French manufacturers or, more simply, the three hundred mentioned above. Even without going into details, however, he would have no hope of getting it all inside the covers of a book of reasonable size. It is necessary, therefore, to make a choice, not only between the manufacturers but also of their different models, with no pretence of being exhaustive. The object of this book is not to give the readers a sort of catalogue of all the cars made in France between 1920 and 1925, but to introduce them to those which, for whatever reason, are worthy of our attention.

Pierre Dumont
June 1977

The Old-Timers

Among the manufacturers who were well established before 1914 and who restarted production after the war, some took a clean sheet of paper and designed completely new models, bearing no relationship to what they had done before. Others, on the contrary, built chassis that were really out of date, even though, in some cases, the layout was of recent conception.

It was the mentality of these manufacturers, the character of their chassis, the more or less obsolete style of their bodywork—and not the date when they began operations—that put them in the class of old-timers. Neither Panhard nor Peugeot, who both started in 1891–2, were in

Coupé-limousine by Rothschild on a 30 cv Delaunay-Belleville chassis

1924: a 30 cv Delaunay-Belleville

A lorry of the greatest luxury: such was the 1922 Delaunay-Belleville whose transmission is shown here

The rear axle of the six-cylinder Delaunay-Belleville, still fitted with twin wheels in 1922

that category, for they knew how to develop and produce modern chassis right from the start of the period covered by this book.

A MAGNIFICENT PAST

The most typical case was, without doubt, Delaunay-Belleville, the producer before 1914 of powerful and sumptuous automobiles, which were the inspiration of certain American manufacturers and gained Royal Appointment to the Court of Imperial Russia. In 1919, Delaunay-Belleville went into production with three chassis taken straight from the 1913 catalogue, which even at that time had not been regarded as technically advanced. There were two six-cylinder models, type K of 78 × 140 mm (4013 cc) and type O of 103 × 160 mm (7999 cc), and a four-cylinder of 100 × 140 mm (4398 cc), with cylinders cast in pairs or blocks of three and naturally with side valves. It was not until somewhat later that Delaunay-Belleville would espouse the monobloc cylinders and overhead valves that were regarded as normal by most other firms, and even then the new models were obviously derived from their forbears. Only the replacement of the very low bonnet and the famous round radiator, by a higher bonnet and a slightly V-fronted, oval radiator, marked the evolution of the robust but heavy Delaunays.

Styled in the fashion of several years before, and often disfigured with huge disc wheels that would have suited a lorry better, at least their engine sizes were more reasonable. They were: four cylinders 10/12 cv 72 × 120 mm (1954 cc), 10/14 cv 70 × 130 mm (2001 cc), 18 cv 100 × 140 mm (4398 cc) and six cylinders 14/16 cv 78 × 140 mm (4013 cc), 25/30 cv 88 × 150 mm (5474 cc).

Also comparable, though in a different category, was the case of Brasier, who were still producing in 1921–2 their old four-cylinder 10 cv 75 × 120 mm (2120 cc), 18 cv 85 × 150 mm (3405 cc), and their vast six-cylinder 30 cv 85 × 150 mm (5107 cc). It was not until the Paris Motor Show of 1922 that the firm which twice won the Gordon-Bennett race (Taunus Circuit 1904, Auvergne Circuit 1905),

Brasier advertisement, October 1921

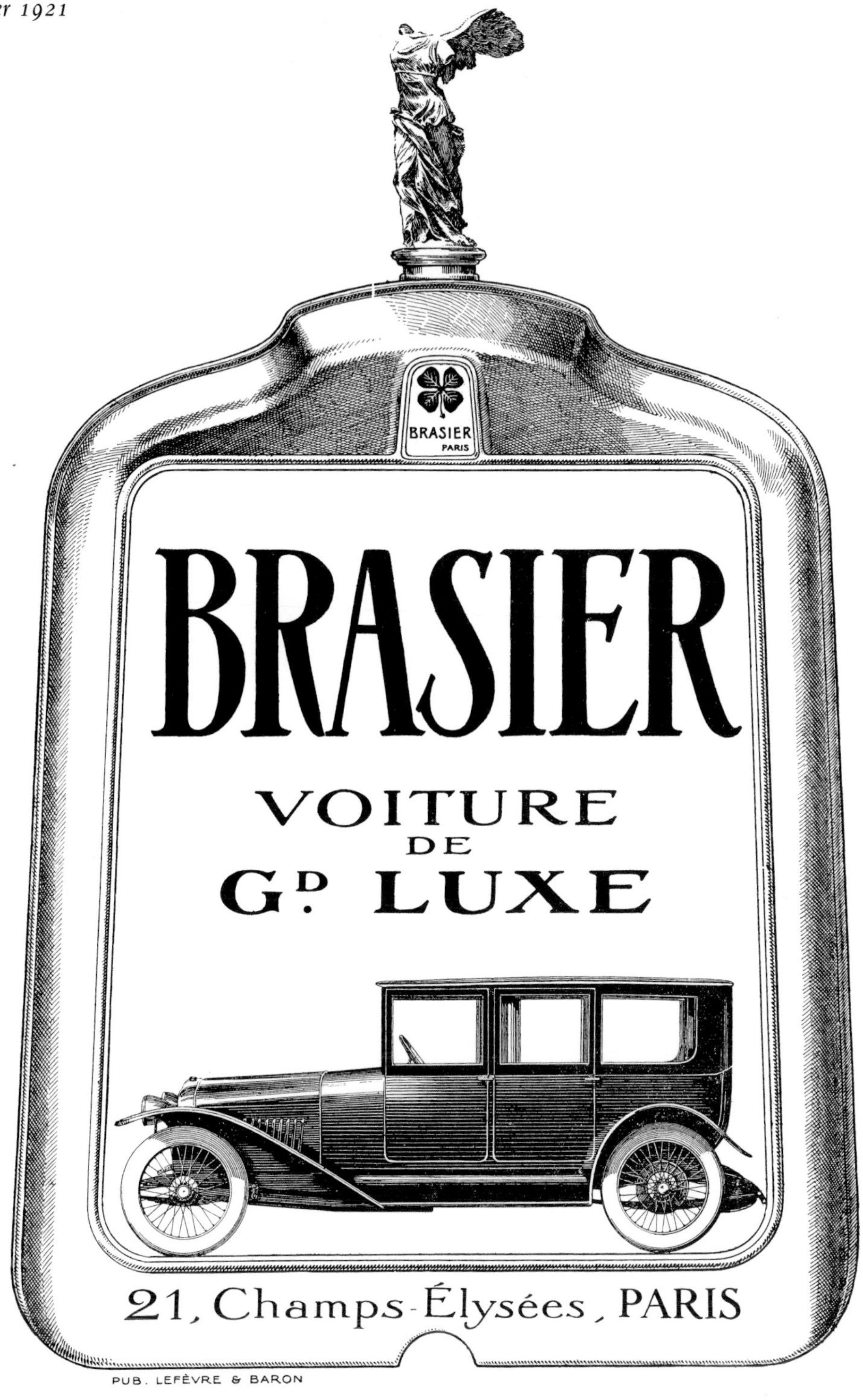

A Brasier of the early twenties: a poor copy of a Voisin, emphasized by the special headlamp mountings

The type TB Brasier chassis, the engine having five main bearings and pushrod-operated overhead valves

The type TBa Brasier engine

Right: 1922 La Licorne advertisement

COMPAGNIE FRANÇAISE DES AUTOMOBILES CORRE

SOCIÉTÉ ANONYME

AU CAPITAL

de 800.000 Francs

"La Licorne"

Adresse Télégraphique :

AUTO-CORRE, Neuilly-sur-Seine

Téléph. : WAGRAM 65-21

Siège social, Usines et Bureaux : 37, Rue de Villiers et 12, Rue de Rouvray -:- NEUILLY-SUR-SEINE

TORPÉDO 2-3 Places (Type M2V)

PRIX ET DESCRIPTION DU CHASSIS NU

CHASSIS type M2V, en tôle emboutie, rétréci à l'avant.
MOTEUR 4 cylindres 65×100. Carburateur horizontal, graissage automatique, magnéto haute tension.
DIRECTION à vis sans fin irréversible. Barre de commande à double amortisseur.
EMBRAYAGE cône cuir.
CHANGEMENT DE VITESSE 3 vitesses avant et marche arrière.
TRANSMISSION par cardan longitudinal.
PONT ARRIERE à fusées creuses porteurs, poussée par les ressorts, 2 freins.
ROUES 5 roues amovibles Michelin 710×90.
PNEUMATIQUES 4 pneumatiques Michelin 710×90, lisses.
OUTILLAGE comprenant : 2 clefs à molette, 1 burette, 1 tournevis, 1 pince universelle, 1 pompe à pneus, 2 démonte-pneus, 1 vilebrequin Michelin.

Prix du Châssis nu . . . . Frs

Ce châssis est construit pour supporter un poids total maximum de 400 kilos, y compris la carrosserie, les accessoires, les ailes, les marchepieds et la charge transportée.

CONDUITE INTÉRIEURE 2-3 Places (Type M2V)

DESCRIPTION ET PRIX DE LA VOITURE COMPLÈTE
TYPE M2V 2-3 PLACES

Carrossée en torpédo 2-3 places, celle de gauche en retrait permettant l'adaptation d'un strapontin devant ce voyageur ; peinture au choix : bleu, vert, gris ou noir ; coffre de dossier derrière le conducteur ; coffre arrière ; capote avec rideaux de côté, parebrise, joues aux ailes avant, tapis, 2 phares, 1 générateur, 2 lanternes avant, 1 lanterne arrière, 1 trompe ; outillage tel que décrit ci-contre.

Prix de la Voiture complète . . . . Frs

Carrossée en conduite Intérieure 2-3 places, celle de gauche en retrait permettant l'adaptation d'un strapontin devant ce voyageur ; peinture au choix : bleu, vert, gris ou noir, coffre de dossier derrière le conducteur, coffre arrière, pare-brise, joues aux ailes avant, tapis-brosse, 2 phares, 1 générateur, 2 lanternes avant, 1 lanterne arrière, 1 trompe, outillage tel que décrit ci-contre.

Prix de la Voiture complète. . . . . Frs

Supplément pour strapontin amovible	Frs	150 »
Supplément pour strapontin fixe	Frs	375 »

TORPÉDO 4 Places (Type Ba-W)

Moteur	Ba W 4 cylindres 65×120.
	Graissage automatique, magnéto blindée, carburateur à pulvérisation.
Radiateur	en coupe-vent, thermosiphon, façade emboutie.
Châssis	tôle emboutie, rétréci à l'avant, cintré à l'arrière (largeur 0.90).
Ressorts	droits, longs, larges, résistants.
Articulations . .	des ressorts, avec boulons graisseurs.
Direction	à vis sans fin irréversible, barre de commande à double amortisseur placée au-dessus du corps de l'essieu.
Embrayage. . . .	cône cuir inverse avec ressort et démarrage progressif.

CONDUITE INTÉRIEURE 4 places (Type Ba-W)

Changement de vitesse . .	3 vitesses avant et marche arrière.
Transmission	par cardan longitudinal.
Pont arrière	à fusées creuses porteurs, poussée par les ressorts.
Roues	5 roues pleines amovibles Michelin 760×90.
Pneumatiques . . .	4 pneus lisses Michelin 760×90.
Réservoir à essence . .	dans l'auvent et d'une capacité de 45 litres environ.
Outillage.	Trousse garnie comprenant 2 clefs à molette, 1 burette, 1 tournevis, 1 pince universelle, 1 pompe à pneus, 2 démonte-pneus, 1 vilebrequin pour démontage des roues.

TYPES	Nombre de cylindres	Puissance nominale	Alésage et course	Nombre de tours	Démarrage	Eclairage	Transmission	Embrayage	Nombre de vitesses	Pneus	Voie	Empattement	Prix du châssis	Prix de la voiture complète	OBSERVATIONS
M2V	4	8	65/100	1500	à volonté	à volonté	Cardan	Cône cuir	3	710×90	1m00	2m600			En châssis. En torpédo 2-3 places Cond. int. 2-3 places
Ba W	4	10	65/120	1500	à volonté	à volonté	Cardan	Cône cuir	3	760×90	1m300	2m900			En châssis. Torpédo 2-3 places, Cond. int. 2-3 places, Torpédo 4 places, Cond. int. 4 places

1922: The chassis of the 10 cv La Licorne. It could equally well be that of any other medium-sized car

The rear axle of the 10 cv La Licorne following the classic principles of the twenties full-length chassis, semi-elliptic springs, friction-type shock absorbers, rod-operated brakes

The side-valve Ballot engine which was fitted to, among others, the 10 cv La Licorne

presented a model in a rather more modern idiom, the type TBa, having a four-cylinder overhead-valve engine of 74 × 120 mm (2094 cc), with five main bearings; it had a single-plate clutch, four-speed gearbox, and servo-assisted brakes on all four wheels.

This car formed the basis of the TC4, a sporting version with two sparking plugs per cylinder, of which two examples were entered for Le Mans in 1923 and 1924. On the first occasion, one retired and the other finished eleventh, while in 1924 they were seventh, at a 76 km/h (47 mph) average, and eighth. The historic and glorious make was taken over in 1926 by Chaigneau, Chaigneau-Brasier being absorbed in its turn by Delahaye in 1930.

Right: 10 cv Unic 1923

The DFP chassis. Note the gearbox separate from the engine, transmission brake, cantilever springs, and forked torque tube anchorage

LITTLE TOURING TRUCKS

Entirely different from these two makes, in the utility class which André Citroën would soon dominate, were two manufacturers, Corre 'La Licorne' (The Unicorn) and Unic, heading a large group.

In 1920, Corre built a small racing car with some original features. Its four-cylinder engine had 16 valves, inclined in the head and operated by pushrods and rockers from two camshafts in the crank-case, the crankshaft running on ballraces. It was rumoured that this advanced power unit was the work of Némorin Causan, the celebrated designer of high-performance engines for Bignan, Buc, La Perle, and others. But the chassis of this little meteor, which was capable of 140 km/h (87 mph), had no front brakes and only a three-speed gearbox, which betrayed a certain conservatism; a conservatism which showed in every detail of the sadly commonplace production models.

One finds, in the 1919 La Licorne catalogue, type BV, 10 cv four cylinders 60 × 110 mm (1244 cc), which was followed in 1920 by the type BaV, 65 × 120 mm (1593 cc), and in 1921 by the type M2V, 65 × 100 mm (1327 cc). In 1921 the BaV became BaW, 65 then 67 × 120 mm (1593 cc, 1693 cc) and all these models had in common a track of 1.30 m (4 ft 3·2 in), with alternative wheelbases of 2·60 m (8 ft 6·4 in) or 2·89 m (9 ft 5·8 in).

Other characteristics included a leather cone clutch and a

A 14 cv DFP open touring car, 1922

Right: the Sigma type V, 1923

Société des AUTOMOBILES SIGMA

AU CAPITAL DE 1.500.000 FRANCS

USINE : 272, Route de la Révolte, 272

LEVALLOIS-PERRET (Seine)

TÉLÉPHONE : 510 LEVALLOIS

Adresse Télégraphique : SIGMA-LEVALLOIS-PERRET

MAGASIN de VENTE : 6, avenue de la Grande Armée

PARIS

TÉLÉPHONE : WAGRAM { 69-17 / 68-83

TORPÉDO, DEUX PLACES
Type Sport

TORPÉDO, QUATRE PLACES

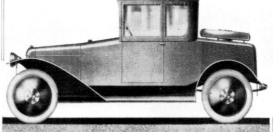

CONDUITE INTÉRIEURE, DEUX PLACES

CONDUITE INTÉRIEURE, QUATRE PLACES

TYPES	Nombre de cylindres	Puissance nominale	Alésage et course	Nombre de tours	Démarrage	Eclairage	Transmission	Embrayage	Nombre de vitesses	Pneus	Voie	Empattement	Prix du châssis	Prix indicatif de la voiture complète	OBSERVATIONS
V	4	9 HP	65 m/m 120 m/m	1.800	Électrique	Électrique	Cardan	Métallique	4 et marche AR	760.90 lisse	1 m 15	2 m 87	Devis sur demande	18.250 19.750 22.000	Torpédo, 4 places, — sport. Conduite intérieure, 2 places — 4 places

The 10 cv Grégoire of 1919

three-speed gearbox, except for a four-speed box on the B7W4, an up-market version of the B4W. In 1923 the La Licorne range was completed with an 11 cv, 70 × 130 mm (2001 cc) car. One ought perhaps to say that all these side-valve engines, as with many other small manufacturers, came from the Ballot factory.

The Unic, with its reputation for never wearing out, might be placed in the same class, except that it was slightly larger and heavier. The Unic, like La Licorne, could as often

be seen equipped as an estate car or pick-up as with an open touring or convertible body, and above all it was well-known as a taxi. In the early 1920s, the manufacturer from Puteaux offered the following range of cars, all with four cylinders; 7/10 cv 75 × 110 mm (1944 cc), 12 cv 75 × 120 mm (2120 cc) (the same size as the 10 cv Brasier and Renault), and 13 cv 80 × 130 mm (2614 cc).

The specification included side valves, a cone clutch (replaced by multiple discs in 1922), and a four-speed

A De Dion V8 engine, as exhibited at L'Espace Cardin

gearbox. The track and wheelbase of the 13 cv type M2T were 1·38 m (4 ft 6·3 in) and 3·20 m (10 ft 6 in) respectively. For 1925, Unic presented the LT, four cylinders 70 × 120 mm (1847 cc), with optional tracks of 1·34 m (4 ft 4·8 in) or 1·41 m (4 ft 7·5 in) and a wheelbase of 3·05 m (10 ft), also the L3T3, 72·8 × 120 mm (2000 cc), with the 1·34 m track and the same wheelbase.

The DFP (Doriot, Flandrin, Parent) and the Suère were both after the same customers and showed a similar conventional technique, innocent of the slightest imagination. DFP, however, had fitted aluminium pistons since 1913, which were developed by their British concessionaire, W. O. Bentley.

Both these manufacturers built four-cylinder, side-valve cars of broadly similar specifications, except that the DFP had a cone clutch and the Suère a disc, though they both had three-speed gearboxes. Typical models were the 10/14 cv

A four-cylinder De Dion shown at the Le Mans museum

DFP of 1919–20, 70 × 130 mm (2001 cc), the type EM of 1922, 65 × 120 mm (1593 cc), and the 10 cv Suère of 1923, 70 × 120 mm (1847 cc). They were homely cars, with no pretence of mechanical sophistication, more akin to beasts of burden than thoroughbreds.

Nevertheless, in 1923 DFP adopted unit construction and front-wheel brakes, developing from their 12 cv a sports model capable of a timed 110km/h (68 mph). After that, the cruel nickname, *Dernière Ferraille Parue*, which may be loosely translated as 'the last word in scrap-iron', was no longer deserved.

The Sigma might also be placed in this group, of which

Right: advertisement for the V8 Darracq

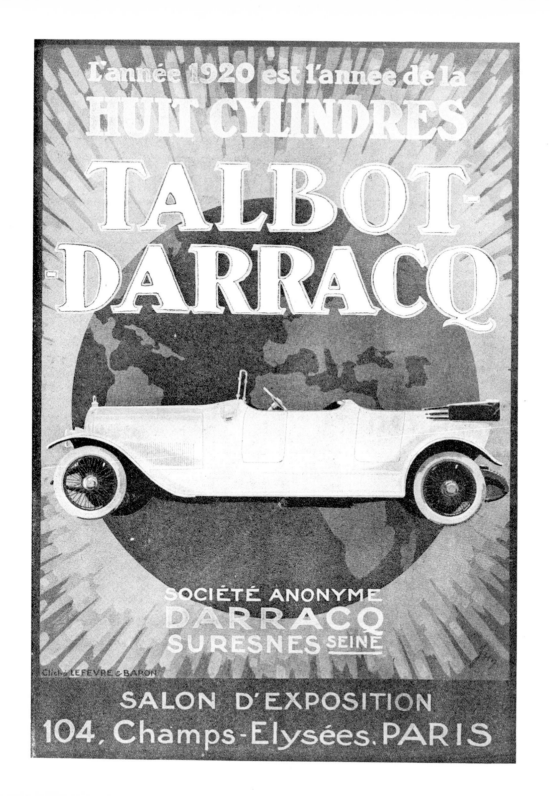

The V8 engine of the Darracq

The gearbox in unit with the engine and the central gear and brake levers of the V8 Darracq: a touch of modernity

the type R, four cylinders 60 × 100 mm (1131 cc), dated from 1913 and was replaced by the type V, 65 × 120 mm (1593 cc). It was a popular car, rather less utilitarian than the DFP, Suère, Unic, or La Licorne, in fact it was more a commercial traveller's or 'rep's' car than that of a farmer, being quite light and of compact size, with a track of 1·15 m (3 ft 9·3 in) and a wheelbase of 2·87 m (9 ft 5 in).

Less commercial and more of a long-distance traveller was the 10 cv Grégoire (but nothing to do with J. A. Grégoire, the front-drive Tracta man), which was manufactured at Poissy long before Simca. Certain details force me to put this new model of 1919 among the old-timers, though it was not without charm and was notable for the impressive output, in relation to its engine size, of 35 bhp, thanks to a compression ratio considered high at that date, of 5 to 1. Four cylinders 70 × 130 mm (2001 cc), with side valves, a cone clutch, and no front brakes—such were the characteristics of this car, built on a chassis with a track and wheelbase of 1·29 m (4 ft 2·8 in) and 2·85 m (9 ft 4·2 in). It was a pity that it looked rather old-fashioned, too.

SOME V8s BEFORE THE AMERICANS

De Dion, Darracq, Bellanger, these were three makes with an important point in common. All three had V8 engines, and two of them had experience in this field extending over a number of years. Better still, Darracq, already holder of the world record for speed in 1904—168 km/h (104 mph) with a four-cylinder 11 litre car—beat that in 1905 at 176 km/h (109 mph) with a V8 of more than 22 litre capacity. De Dion, on the other hand, had the first genuine production engine of this type, which incidentally gave the idea to the American engineers.

While the 200 hp Darracq engine of 1905 had pushrod-operated overhead valves, the production V8 of 1919–20 was designed, like the De Dion, on conventional lines. Only that of Bellanger had overhead valves, despite which it was short of breath. For the rest, the chassis of these three cars were on completely classical lines—that's the least one can say—the

Bellanger's needing two pairs of front springs to support it. As for their bodies, there was nothing exciting about those.

In the case of De Dion, let us make an exception and dip into the past. In 1910, the first V8s of the impetuous Marquis and little Mr. Bouton were types CN, 75 × 100 mm (3534 cc), and CJ, 90 × 120 mm (6107 cc). In 1911 there was the CY, 90 × 140 mm (7125 cc), and then in 1912 the types DM, 70 × 130 mm (4002 cc) and DN, 94 × 140 mm (7772 cc), which was to become EF, EY, FM and then GO. In 1913, the 75 × 130 mm (4594 cc) EC later became ED, while a 66 × 130 mm (3558 cc) received the designations of ER and then ES, whereupon type FA appeared, 75 × 120 mm (4241 cc). One asks oneself what modifications might have corresponded with all those type letters, or what commercial gains could have justified so many different cylinder capacities.

The clumsy appearance of a four-cylinder Bellanger

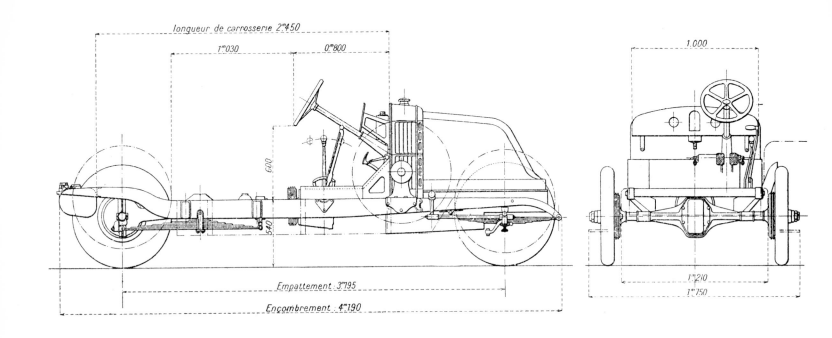

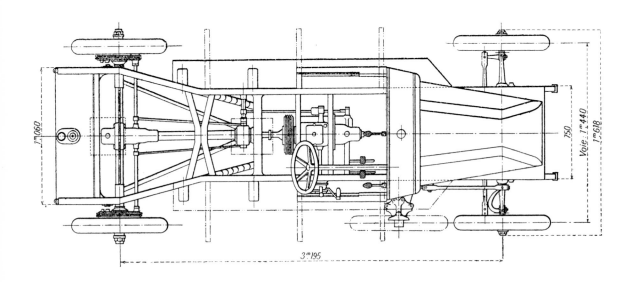

The chassis of the 12 cv Renault: the 1914 concept of the design is obvious

24

A 1921 12 cv Renault open touring car: ten years behind the times but sturdy and quite pleasant to drive. 60 bhp and 90 km/h (56 mph)

There came in due course, in 1919, types GR, 66 × 130 mm, GS, 75 × 130 mm, and HS/HT, 94 × 140 mm, then in 1920 types MG, 70 × 120 mm (3694 cc), and IB, 65 × 100 mm (2654 cc). This whole range, of a variety that could scarcely be imagined except at this epoch, was replaced at the end of 1923 by a series of overhead-valve four-cylinder cars, composed of the following models: IS and IT, 70 × 120 mm (1847 cc), with a wheelbase of 2·97 m (9 ft 8·9 in) and IW, the long-wheelbase version, 3·09 m (10 ft 1·3 in); IM, 78 × 130 mm (2484 cc); JK, 95 × 140 mm (3969 cc).

Types IS and IT were developed from type IC with the same bore and stroke, the old 10 cv of many years standing, dating even from before the V8 era, when it was the largest

The standard Renault 18 cv chassis: every feature emphasizes that the design concept goes back many years

A Renault 18 cv limousine of 1919

De Dion made. It had a side-valve engine with a two-bearing crankshaft, no front brakes and long, cantilever rear springs. The 10 cv, like the models that came after it, was what people call a good tool, rugged but without much personality.

Parallel with the type A side-valve V8, 75 × 130 mm (4594 cc), Darracq went back into production, after the war, with the 12/14 cv, four cylinders 85 × 130 mm (2951 cc). Whereas the V8 had a multiple-disc clutch, the smaller car

was fitted with a cone, but they both had four-speed gearboxes and shared a track of 1·35 m (4 ft 3·1 in), with wheelbases of 3·50 m (11 ft 5·8 in) and 3·15 m (10 ft 4 in).

The heavy type F Bellanger 35/50 cv V8, 90 × 125 mm (6362 cc), had a track of 1·42 m (4 ft 7·9 in) and a wheelbase of 3·75 m (12 ft 3·6 in) and in addition, there were two four-cylinder models, also with overhead valves. Type A1 15/17 cv, 90 × 125 mm (3181 cc), had a three-speed gearbox and a

28

An open touring body by Kellner on the light 18 cv chassis of 1920: the high frame and odd bonnet do not facilitate the coachbuilder's task

track of 1·42 m, with a short wheelbase of 2·76 m (9 ft 0·6 in), while the type D 24/30 cv, 95 × 150 mm (4253 cc), had four speeds, a 1·42 m track like the other two, and a wheelbase of 3·75 m (12 ft 1·6 in). Once again, the general conception of the Bellangers, their design, their heavy and unfashionable appearance, and particularly their lack of performance (this last did not apply to De Dions or Darracqs), placed them far behind other contemporary makes that were truly modern.

MEANWHILE AT BILLANCOURT

The post-war Renaults closely resembled the pre-1914 models; even the brand new 10 cv, of which we shall make the acquaintance a little farther on, was already dated at the time of its birth. This last chassis excepted, Louis Renault's range for 1920 was as follows.

The type EK two cylinders, 80 × 120 mm (1206 cc), direct descendant of the taxis of the Marne, otherwise known

A 40 cv long chassis Renault, with coachwork by Jean Gaborit, 1923

as the '*deux pattes*' (two paws) of 1907–8.

The type JM 12 cv four cylinders, 80 × 140 mm (2815 cc), developed from the type EV of 1917 and available in two forms, normal chassis or low chassis. It had a track of 1·40 m (4 ft 7·1 in) and a wheelbase of 3·10 m (10 ft 2 in) for the normal chassis, 3·34 m (10 ft 11 in) for the low chassis, reduced to 3·19 m (10 ft 5·6 in) on the last examples.

The 18 cv four cylinders, 95 × 160 mm (4536 cc), was derived from types ED of 1913, EI of 1914, and FE of 1917. The track and wheelbase were 1·50 m (4 ft 11 in) and 3·63 m (11 ft 9 in) for the normal model, 1·40 m (4 ft 7·1 in) and 3·30 m (10 ft 9·9 in) for the light model.

The 40 cv six cylinders, 100 × 160 mm (7540 cc), had a track of 1·50 m (4 ft 11 in) and a wheelbase of 3·54 m (11 ft 7·4 in) or 3·91 m (12 ft 9·9 in). The bore was soon increased to 110 mm, giving a capacity of 9123 cc.

Renault: an 18 cv of 1924, or the 40 cv in miniature

On the 12 cv and on the 40 cv, the rear suspension was by oblique cantilever springs and on the 18 cv by classic semi-elliptics. It was only on the 10cv that the transverse rear spring was found which would later become standard on the great majority of chassis from Billancourt. All the models naturally retained the radiator behind the engine, traditional with Renault, and the bonnet identical with that of the pre-war cars, called coalscuttle or pig's snout, which was to be replaced in 1923 by the 'new' bonnet with sharp angles. The four-cylinder 12 and 18 cv disappeared then, too, to be superseded by a six-cylinder 15 cv 'standard' and six-cylinder 15 cv and 18 cv 'de luxe'.

These last two may be considered as reduced versions of the 40 cv, while the 15 cv 'standard' was like a bigger 10 cv. Surpassed right from its birth by competitors of more modern design, the 40 cv Renault, which descended in a straight line from models prior to 1914, was none the less an automobile of very great luxury and comparable, except in mechanical sophistication, with the most refined. It was also, if the necessity arose, an extremely fast car. It only needed a suitable axle ratio and a light body, and the huge engine would do the rest, as was twice proved on the Montlhéry track. In 1925, an open sports four-seater, like any customer's car except for the removal of the mudguards, plus a very high-geared crown wheel and pinion, covered 3384 km in 24 hours, an average of 141 km/h (88 mph). The next year, a rather more special 40 cv, with a streamlined body, modified radiator, and an even higher gear, broke its own 24 hours record at an average speed of 176 km/h (109 mph), with a fastest lap at 193 km/h (120 mph).

A NAME FOR DAYS TO COME

There remains Delahaye which, for sentimental reasons, I would have loved to classify among the 'moderns'. Alas, there were the type 64N 12/16 cv of 1919 and type 84 14/18 cv, four cylinders 85 × 130 mm (2951 cc), with a track of 1·36 m (4 ft 5·5 in) and a wheelbase of 3·23 m (10 ft 7·2 in) or 3·39 m (11 ft 1·5 in). There were type 82 18/22 cv, six cylinders 85 × 130 mm (4426 cc), with a wheelbase of 3·67 m (12 ft 0·5 in), and type 87 10 cv, four cylinders 70 × 120 mm (1847 cc), which was presented at the 1921 Paris Motor Show. It had a fixed-head, side-valve engine, a cone clutch, and brakes only on the rear hubs and transmission. It was fairly lively and of very robust build but, in spite of its unit construction, it was of obsolescent design.

Alone there emerges from the whole range the type 94 of 1922–3, a 15 cv four-cylinder with the bore and stroke of the type 84, but with overhead valves. Did it foretell, more than ten years beforehand, the Superluxe and the type 135, which were to bring glory to the old make from the rue du Banquier?

A sports-touring 40 cv Renault from Henri Malartre's collection. The round emblem was soon replaced by the 'lozenge'

The 40 cv of the 1925 records, type MC long chassis, with body by Lavocat et Marsaud. This is not the same one as was used in the first tests, which was crashed. The body was similar but the registration number was different and that car had wire wheels

The driving seat of the 40 cv Renault. By whom or for what purpose can the door be used?

The 10 cv Vinot-Deguingand of 1923 is the archetype of certain cars that were technically sound but clumsily bodied

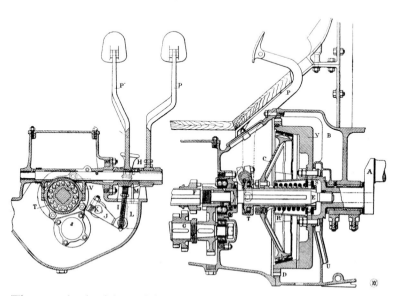

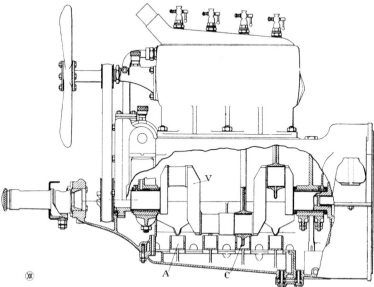

The cone clutch of the Delahaye

Two views of the Delahaye engine with its non-detachable cylinder head

At the Delahaye Retrospective of 1975: two type 87s, 1920 below,
1923 on the right

Some Modern Conceptions

With the war of 1914–18 over, most of the established motor manufacturers revised their ideas, to adapt them to the new conditions in the production and use of vehicles. As for those who were newly entering the industry, generally after four years of armament work and especially aircraft construction, it was only natural that they should adopt modern techniques, with very few exceptions.

It is, admittedly, very difficult to give a precise definition of the two tendencies, ancient and modern, and to fix boundaries which will permit a strict classification. Some manufacturers managed for a while to steer a middle course, but others followed a mixture of old-fashioned and novel doctrines in the same design; a third group compromised by producing a frankly conservative model and an advanced one, alongside each other.

Having said that, one notes among the modern tendencies:

—research into the lightening of the whole chassis;

—simplification of design, affecting the engine as well as the chassis;

—regrouping of the main components (analogous to the substitution of a monobloc casting for single or paired cylinders) the engine, clutch, and gearbox were combined in a single unit;

—the general adoption of brakes on all four wheels;

—research into higher specific outputs at greater crankshaft speeds, with lighter moving parts, all made possible by the latest developments in metallurgy;

—improvements in carburation and in methods of valve operation, notably the replacement of side by overhead camshaft (twin camshafts were still only for racing), also sleeve valves;

—the evolution of cars that were easier to drive, with smoother clutches, usually single disc instead of cone, and gearboxes directly controlled by a central lever;

—more elegant coachwork on lower chassis, with simpler lines and better proportions, giving improved comfort to the passengers, including the beginning of the general adoption of closed bodies.

QUICKLY AND SILENTLY, SHE PASSES . . .

Such was the advertising slogan used during this period by Delage, who always produced cars built according to the principles stated above after 1920. We shall also meet Delage later on, when we cover the racing cars. Starting in 1905 with a preference for small-engined vehicles, Louis Delage went over to four cylinders in 1908, using proprietary power units from De Dion, Chapuis-Dornier, and Ballot, before building his own from 1910 onwards. He had made a name for his cars in racing before 1914 and, in 1916–17, he started preparations for the manufacture of a fine luxury car after the war.

Called type CO, it was designed by engineer Lovera, who had come from Fiat, and it had a six-cylinder engine of quite moderate size for the epoch, 80 × 150 mm (4524 cc), developing 65/68 bhp. It had a track of 1·44 m (4 ft 8·7 in)

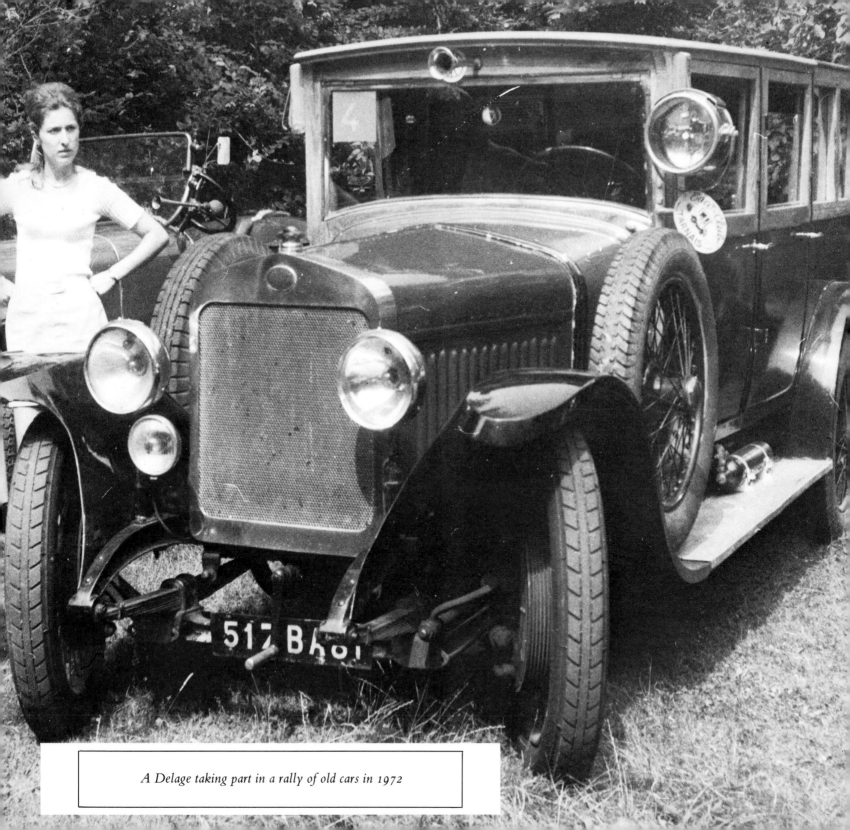

A Delage taking part in a rally of old cars in 1972

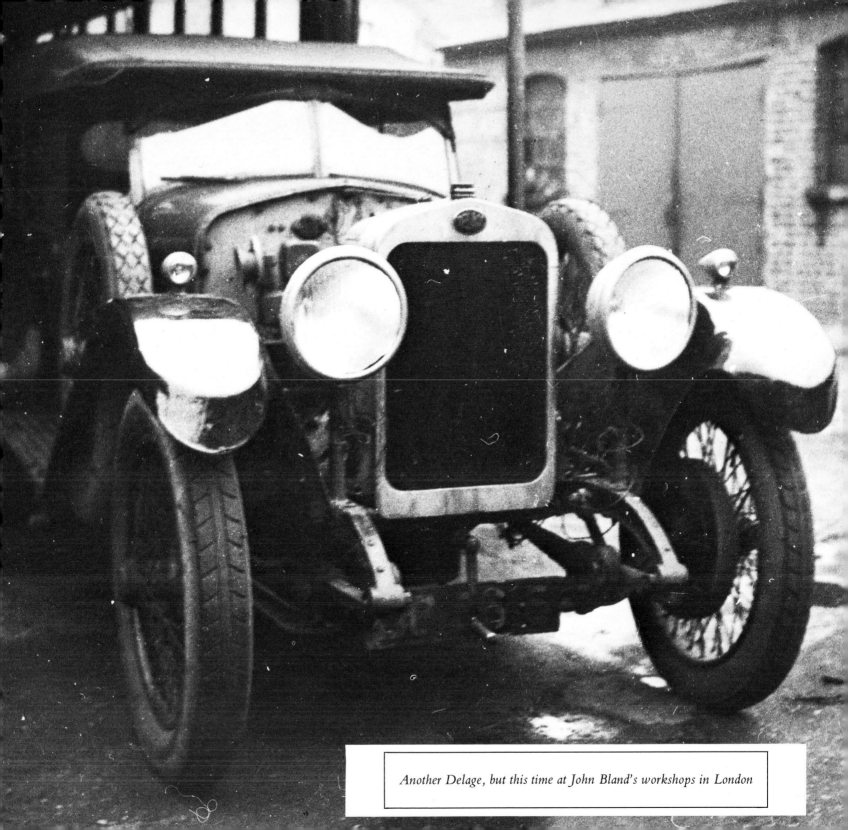

Another Delage, but this time at John Bland's workshops in London

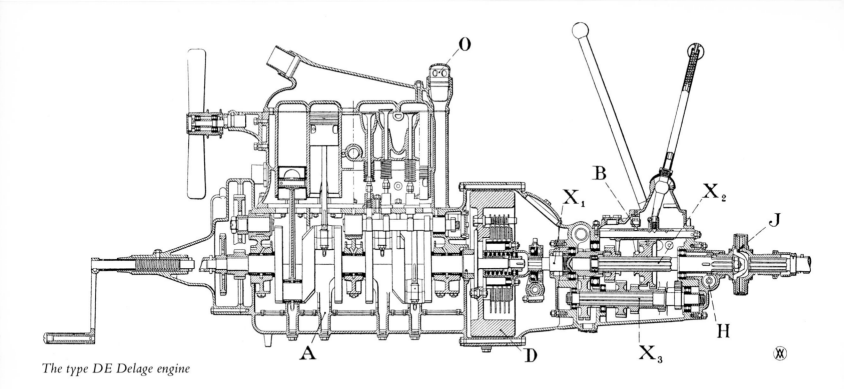

The type DE Delage engine

and alternative wheelbases of 3·43 m (11 ft 3 in) or 3·86 m (12 ft 0·9 in), which gave sufficient space for beautiful and comfortable coachwork.

The presentation was at the Paris Motor Show of 1919. Accompanied by the journalist, W. F. Bradley, Louis Delage drove from Paris to Nice at an average of 67 km/h (42 mph), which greatly assisted the promotion of the new model. Two years later the CO became the GS (Grand Sport) when it received an overhead-valve cylinder head which was good for 80 bhp, but in 1923 it was called type CO2 instead, with no further changes in specification.

At the Paris Show of 1920, Delage presented the DO, with four cylinders of the same bore and stroke as the CO, making 3016 cc. This was taxed at 15/16 cv, developing 43 bhp, again with a track of 1·44 m (4 ft 8·7 in) and a wheelbase of 3·18 m (10 ft 5·2 in) or 3·42 m (11 ft 2·6 in). In 1921, a smaller side-valve four-cylinder, the DE, was added to the range, with dimensions of 72 × 130 mm (2117 cc), taxed at 11 cv and developing 32 bhp; the track was 1·32 m

(4 ft 3·9 in) and the wheelbase 2·98 m (9 ft 9·3 in) or 3·18 m (10 ft 5·2 in). With this small machine Louis Delage, accompanied by his son, Pierre, performed an impressive publicity stunt. Leaving Paris, he drove to twelve large cities, including Geneva and Brussels with the others spread over France, but to increase the distance, he returned to Paris and left again after visiting each one. This added up to 8500 km (5282 miles) at an average of over 50 km/h (31 mph).

In 1922, Louis Delage had two prototypes built, called type 2LS (2 Litre Sport), with four-cylinder engines of 70 × 130 mm (2001 cc), developing no less than 75 bhp, of which the overhead-valve cylinder head was the work of Toutée, the celebrated designer of Chenard-Walcker and Ariès engines. It is likely that the cylinder bores were left undersize at about 69·5 mm, an accepted dimension for the popular two-litre competition class.

It was in 1923 that the DI made its appearance. The overhead-valve, four-cylinder engine had dimensions of 75 × 120 mm (2121 cc) with a fiscal rating of 11 cv, which

The DE chassis, just as well designed as the engine

An 18 cv Hotchkiss open touring car of 1921. The rear suspension by cantilever springs, well shown here, was often used on luxury cars of the epoch

Delage: the type DO engine . . .

Hotchkiss: the rear suspension of the type AK . . .

. . . and the GS engine: a similar elegance of design

. . . and the engine of the type AM

developed 30 bhp. The track was 1·32 m (4 ft 3·9 in) and the wheelbase 3·18 m (10 ft 5·2 in), but there was also the DIC (Coloniale) model, with a higher chassis and a wider track of 1·42 m (4 ft 7·9 in). Some sporting versions of the DI, incorporating experience gained with the 2LS, were the DIS (Sport) and the low-chassis DISS (Sport Surbaissé), and later the DI5 and DI6.

In 1924, when production of the CO had ceased, Delage brought out a new six-cylinder luxury automobile, the GL, of 95 × 140 mm (5954 cc). It had a track of 1·48 m (4 ft 10·3 in) and a wheelbase of 3·62 m (11 ft 10·5 in) or 3·85 m (12 ft 7·6 in),

THE GOLDEN MEAN

Some French phrases almost defy translation, but for the Hotchkiss advertising slogan, *Le Juste Milieu*, perhaps 'The Golden Mean' is as near as one can get. When the activities of Hotchkiss restarted, the first productions were four pre-war models, the 12/16 cv, 18/22 cv, and 20/30 cv, all with four cylinders, plus a six-cylinder 20/30 cv. They had side-valve engines with non-detachable cylinder heads, but only the 18/22 was built in appreciable numbers, first as type AF, then AH and AL, with various modifications.

Hotchkiss, 1923. Poise, decorum, and pleasing proportions: 'The Golden Mean'

The greatest post-war novelty, in 1921 was the type AK, built to the design of Maurice Sainturat. It had a six-cylinder, overhead-camshaft engine of 100 × 140 mm (6597 cc), a similar specification to that of the Hispano-Suiza. This model, which remained in the prototype stage, had a remarkably early example of rising-rate rear suspension, using two pairs of cantilever springs and a system of levers.

but there was also a sports model, the GLS, with the quite reasonable chassis size of 1·40 m (4 ft 7·1 in) × 3·40 m (11 ft 1·9 in) and a more highly-tuned engine, giving 130 bhp instead of the standard 100 bhp output. The overhead-camshaft engine of the GL was designed by Maurice Sainturat, who had worked for Delaunay-Belleville and Hotchkiss and was to be the author of the 7 cv Citroën engine ten years later.

At the 1922 Paris Show, Hotchkiss unveiled the 12 cv four-cylinder, side-valve type AM, 80 × 120 mm (2413 cc), developing a useful 45 bhp. It had a single-disc clutch, a four-speed gearbox, and four-wheel brakes, with a track of 1·35 m (4 ft 5·1 in) and a wheelbase of 3·07 m (10 ft 0·9 in). With the AM, Hotchkiss had found their Golden Mean, an avocation which was to be endorsed in 1925 by the improved AM2.

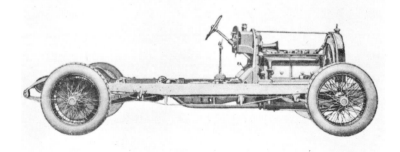

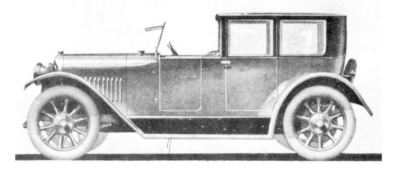

1924, the Lorraine-Dietrich chassis: from top to bottom the 15 cv long, the 15 cv extra-long, and the 30 cv

Three body styles on the 12 cv Lorraine: touring car, saloon, and coupé-limousine

47

Second and third in the 24 Hours race at Le Mans in 1924, first and third in 1925, the Lorraines finished first, second, and third in 1926

The overall dimensions of the Ballot two-litre sports chassis

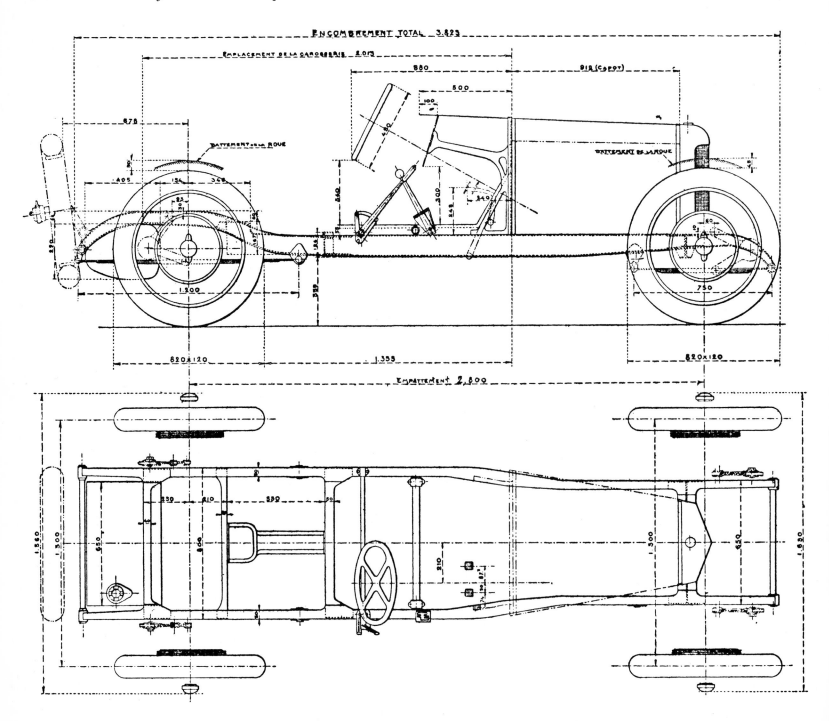

Ballot: overall dimensions of the touring two litre

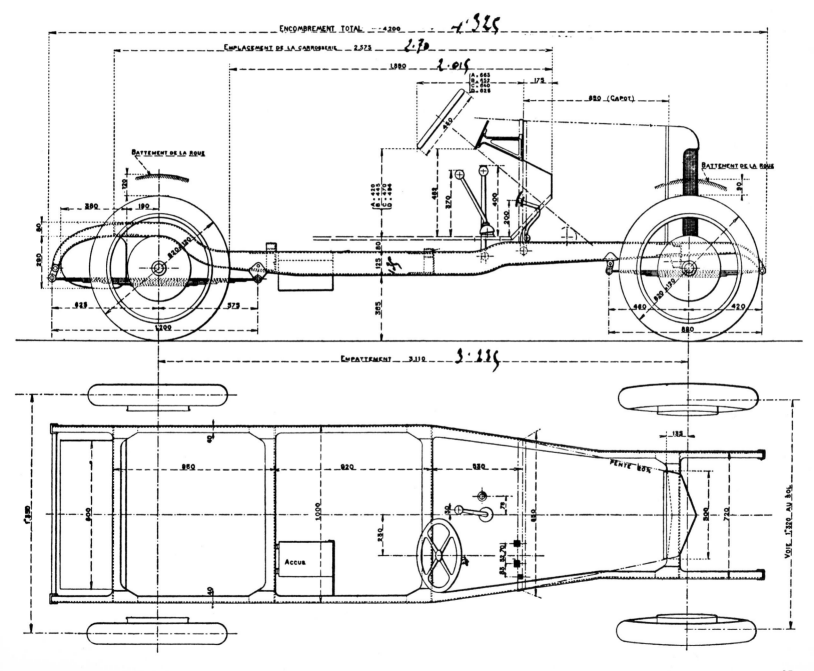

Ballot: the chassis and the engine of the touring two litre. Need one remark on the cleanness of the design?

FROM LUNEVILLE TO ARGENTEUIL

Lorraine-Dietrich, a firm of iron-founders going back to the time of Louis XIV—who was one of their customers—built their first car in 1897 to Amédée Bollée's design. Ettore Bugatti worked for them during his formative years and they raced the last of the 15-litre monsters, before the Peugeots, designed by Henry, made them obsolete.

In 1920, the great house of Lorraine-Dietrich, with factories at Luneville and Argenteuil, was making a six-cylinder 15 cv car of 75 × 130 mm (3446 cc), with overhead valves, called type A1-6. Two larger six-cylinder models were also catalogued, a 20 cv of 80 × 150 mm (4524 cc) and the big D2 of over six-litre capacity. To these, a smaller 12 cv four-cylinder car, the A4, was soon added, of 75 × 130 mm

(2297 cc). Its chassis dimensions were 1·40 m (4 ft 7·1 in) × 2·95 m (9 ft 8·1 in), those of the 15 cv 1·40 m × 2·85 m (9 ft 4·2 in) later 2·90 m (9 ft 6·2 in), and of the D2 1·42 m (4 ft 7·9 in) × 3·33 m (10 ft 11·1 in).

The A1-6 became the B2-6 and, in 1923, the B3-6, with a wheelbase of 3·04 m (9 ft 11·7 in) or 3·25 m (10 ft 8 in), and it was from this last model that a short chassis of 2·89 m (9 ft 5·8 in) was developed in 1924, with dual ignition and twin carburettors. Entered at Le Mans in 1924, three Lorraines came second and third with one retirement, and they dominated the 24 hour race in 1926, finishing in the first three places; they were attaining 150 km/h (93 mph) on the straights, with an overall average of 106 km/h (66 mph). The engine had a non-detachable head with exposed pushrods and was designed by engineer Barbarou, who came from Delaunay-Belleville, like so many others.

THREE FAMOUS TRAVELLERS

Fast, reliable, and silent, the Lorraine was always on the heavy side, with a slightly elderly demeanour, which admittedly did not prevent it, in its sporting form, from winning at Le Mans. Lighter, more prepossessing and vivacious were the Ballots, the Bignans, the Georges Irats, which were the other great travellers of sporting reputation in the twenties.

At the end of the 1914 war, Edouard Ballot, who had for many years manufactured marine engines and power units for cars, such as the Delage and La Licorne, decided to enhance his firm's name by adventuring into the world of competition; we shall see a little later how he fared. From a two-litre racing car with four cylinders, 69·9 × 130 mm, which had sixteen valves operated by twin overhead camshafts in a non-detachable head, Ballot developed a magnificent sports car, the 2LS, which he built in small numbers during 1921–4. It had a cone clutch, a separate four-speed gearbox, brakes on all four wheels, with track and wheelbase of 1·30 m (4 ft 3·2 in) × 2·80 m (9 ft 2·2 in) respectively.

Right: a Ballot at the Fête of the Marguerite at Vésinet

For 1923, Ballot prepared a touring car of sporting tendencies, the 2LT, of which the engine had the same dimensions as the 2LS but all resemblance ended there. It had a single overhead camshaft, driven by a vertical shaft in front, which operated eight parallel valves in a detachable cylinder head, while the crankshaft bearings were plain white-metal instead of rollers. The engine and the four-speed gearbox were in unit, with a single disc clutch, and the chassis dimensions were 1.32 m (4 ft 3.9 in) and 3.25 m (10 ft 8 in). The 2LT was replaced in 1925 by the 2LTS, which was virtually identical except that the valves were inclined and operated by rockers from the overhead camshaft.

In this same class, of the two-litre fast touring cars, we must place the Georges Irat. It had four cylinders, 70 × 130 mm (2001 cc), a detachable cylinder head with pushrod-operated overhead valves, and three main bearings. The clutch was of the multiple disc type, the gearbox had four speeds and there were brakes on all four wheels; the track was 1.30 m (4 ft 3.2 in) and the wheelbase 3.00 m (9 ft 10.1 in). The Georges Irat was a good design, of excellent construction, exceeding 100 km/h (62 mph) against the stopwatch, in 1921.

Our third brilliant two litre car, the Bignan, had an advanced overhead-camshaft, four-cylinder engine with two sparking plugs per cylinder, with the dimensions 75 × 112 mm (1979 cc). This engine was expensive and the car was also available with proprietary units, such as the overhead-camshaft SCAP, 70 × 110 mm (1693 cc), or even a side-valve Ballot, 67 × 120 mm (1693 cc). When fitted with the Bignan engine, this was a very formidable car, for it was closely derived from the one that ran in the touring category of the 1922 Strasbourg Grand Prix; it retired there, but later won its class at Spa. The competition engine was also of 75 × 112 mm (1979 cc) but the valves had positive closing as well as opening on the desmodromic system, with a 70 bhp output that was good for 140 km/h (87 mph).

A sports two-litre Ballot (below) and two touring two-litre models (right)

1922: an open touring Georges Irat

Bignan production had begun in 1919 with the 132C or 17 cv Sport, which had a side-valve, four-cylinder engine, 85 × 130 mm (2951 cc), developing 50 bhp. It appeared at the Paris Show of 1920 with the engine bored out to 92 × 130 mm (3457 cc), when it was renamed 1300 short or 1400 long, with respective wheelbases of 3·01 m (9 ft 10·5 in) and 3·31 m (10 ft 10·3 in).

Bignan ran in the Coupe des Voiturettes at Le Mans in 1920, using engines dating from 1914 with side valves in T-heads, operated by two camshafts in the crank-case. They won the Tour de Corse in 1921 with a 3 litre car, the engine of which had originally been a 2·5 litre pre-war side-valve, but was converted to a 16-valve overhead-camshaft unit under the watchful eye of the brilliant Causan.

One might also mention that an early Bignan production was a 7 cv which, almost to the radiator, was an 1100 cc Salmson of the one rocker per cylinder type.

The engine of the 11 cv Georges Irat

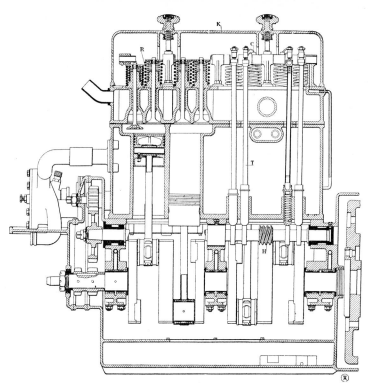

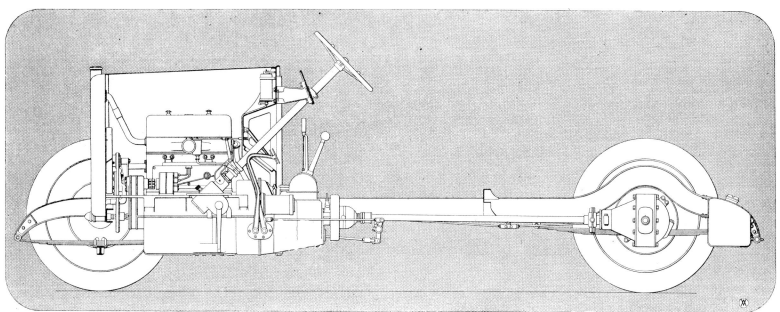

*1922: the chassis of the two-litre Georges Irat. Its elegance is
a far cry from pre-war chassis . . . and from certain contemporary models*

Notre type "Trés sport"

GEORGES
IRAT

100 Kil à l'heure
10 litres d'essence
2 ans de garantie

A touring Bignan of 1923: a poor imitation of Rolls-Royce styling

*Left: an advertisement for the two-litre Georges Irat, in connection
with the Paris Motor Show of 1922*

Strasbourg 1922: the Bignan 'Desmo'

The engine of the 10 cv Talbot DC

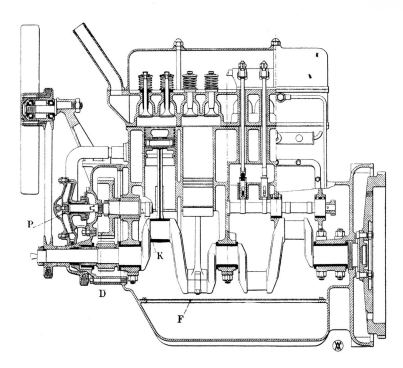

AN ENGLISH CAR AT SURESNES

The story of Talbot is surely one of the most confused that exists. The make was a continuation of that created by Alexandre Darracq at the beginning of the century and which was the basis of the English consortium, STD, otherwise known as Sunbeam-Talbot-Darracq. The Sunbeam firm was directed by a Frenchman, Louis Coatalen, the French branch at Suresnes was controlled by an Englishman, Owen Clegg, while a Swiss, Georges Roesch, designed the English Talbots. Also, an Italian, Bertarione, created some of the racing cars of the group—those which ran sometimes under the name of Talbot and at other times as Sunbeams. You follow me? Good . . .

It is scarcely astonishing that the Talbots of the 1920s, succeeding the Talbot-Darracqs, formerly Darracqs—during which period A. Lago, an Italian, left his directorship at Sunbeam to take over Talbot at Suresnes—had a fairly marked British character. The 10 cv, type DC, had a pushrod engine with three main bearings, dimensions 68 × 110 mm (1598 cc). The clutch had a single disc, the gearbox was of

three speeds, and there were cantilever rear springs; the track was 1·25 m (4 ft 1·2 in) and the wheelbase 3·00 m (9 ft 10·1 in).

Without attaining quite the class of a Ballot, a Georges Irat, or a Bignan, the 10 cv Talbot was a very pleasant touring car, both lively and responsive. These qualities were emphasized when, in 1925, it received the designation DD to signify a small increase in engine size, 69·5 × 110 m (1669 cc), the adoption of a four-speed gearbox, and the addition of four-wheel brakes. The rather narrow wheel track was sensibly increased to 1·35 m (4 ft 5·1 in), the wheelbase becoming 3·11 m (10 ft 2·4 in).

A SMALL CLOUD OF BLUE SMOKE

Some manufacturers sought—and obtained—high power output, flexibility and silence, at the price of a certain increase in oil consumption, by using sleeve valves. Among these were Mors, Peugeot, Voisin, and Panhard. Mors, put back on their feet by André Citroën before 1914, ran into new difficulties after the war. These were due to the destruction of

Talbot DC, 1923/4: the coupé de ville

1924: a Talbot DC with a Weymann body

Talbot DD: the standard saloon

12/16 cv Mors: the engine, exhaust side

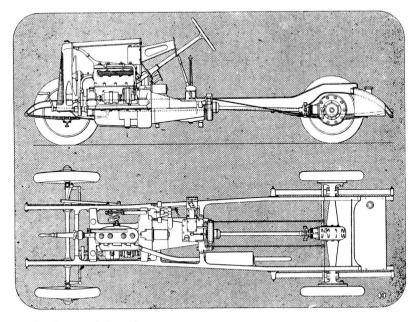

The chassis of the 12/16 Mors

the Minerva factory in Belgium, which supplied their engines. So, it was not until 1922 that the old firm was back in its stride ... to close its doors finally a year later. The last Mors model was the 12/16 cv, having four cylinders and sleeve valves, with dimensions of 75 × 112 mm (1979 cc). The engine was of Minerva design but assembled in Paris, and this car still retained the curious ribbon-type clutch that was peculiar to Mors.

The production of sleeve-valve Peugeots, at the Issy-les-Moulineaux factory, stretched from 1921 to 1929, with five types of touring and sporting chassis. These were:

—type 156, six cylinders 95 × 130 mm (5529 cc), built during 1921–3 to a design that was obsolescent even at its introduction, with twin rear wheels, track 1·45 m (4 ft 10·3 in) and wheelbase 3·67 m (12 ft 0·5 in);

—type 174 or 18 cv, four cylinders 95 × 135 mm (3828 cc), built 1922–8, track 1·43 m (4 ft 8·3 in) and wheelbase 3·50 m (11 ft 5·8 in);

—type 174S or 18 cv Sport, with an engine giving 85 instead of 70 bhp and a shorter wheelbase of 3·27 m (10 ft 8·7 in), plus some more or less highly-tuned competition chassis;

—type 176 or 12/14 cv, four cylinders 80 × 124 mm (2493 cc) developing 55 bhp, which was built in 1923–8, with a track of 1·37 m (4 ft 5·9 in) and a wheelbase of 3·27 m (10 ft 8·7 in);

—type 184, six cylinders 80 × 125 mm (3770 cc) developing 80 bhp, built 1928–9, with a track of 1·43 m (4 ft 8·3 in) and a wheelbase of 3·60 m (11 ft 9·7 in).

The greatest sleeve-valve Peugeot was the 18 cv. It ran in the 1922 Strasbourg Grand Prix (touring category), three months before it went on sale, competing with its half-sister the 18 cv Voisin. It won its class in 1923 at the Grand Prix of the Automobile Club de France on the Tours circuit, did the same in 1924 at the GP of the ACF at Lyons, and dominated the touring category of the 1925 GP of the ACF at Montlhéry, among other successes. In competition form, it came sixth in the Targa Florio and won the Spa Grand Prix in 1926, as well as the Twelve Hours of San Sebastian in 1927.

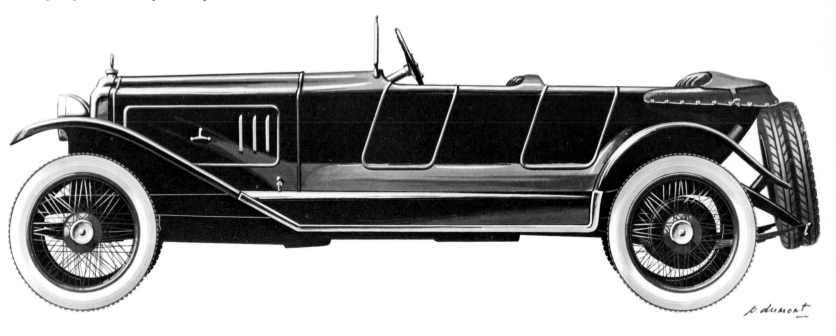

And of course there was Voisin. The first model was developed from a prototype designed in 1917–18 by Artaut, Dufresne and Cabaillot for André Citroën, before the latter decided to concentrate on the mass production of popular cars. Dufresne, the sleeve-valve specialist, came from Panhard and was responsible a little later for the 18 cv Peugeot. Those are the bare facts.

Gabriel Voisin, the celebrated aircraft manufacturer, entered the world of automobiles with the type M or 18 cv, called ADC when it was a Citroën prototype. The engine was built under the Knight patents, with two concentric sleeves per cylinder, which had little connecting rods to eccentrics on a half-speed shaft. This was an arrangement already seen on Panhards, which was also about to appear on Peugeots. The Voisin had four cylinders, 95 × 140 mm (3969 cc), a single disc clutch, four-speed gearbox, and dimensions for track and wheelbase of 1·41 m (4 ft 7·5 in) × 3·46 m (11 ft 4·2 in).

At first with cantilever rear springs, it later had semi-elliptics, when the designation was changed to type C1. In 1921, a variation, called C3 short, had a wheelbase of 3·34 m

(10 ft 11·4 in) and in 1922 the C3 long appeared, 3·57 m (11 ft 8·5 in), followed by the C5 in 1923, which was a C3 short with sporting characteristics. During this period, a team of three Voisins, described as C3 Sport, were entered for the 1922 Strasbourg Grand Prix and took the first three places in the touring category, in front of the 18 cv Peugeots.

There also existed, in 1921, the type C2, which remained a prototype, having 12 cylinders in a very narrow V, with dimensions of 80 × 120 mm (7238 cc). Also Voisin entered some two-litre sleeve-valve cars of highly original design in the Grand Prix of the ACF in 1923. With six-cylinder engines of 62 × 110 mm (1993 cc) which developed 70 bhp, they had a wide front track of 1·45 m (4 ft 9 in), an extremely narrow rear track of 0·75 m (2 ft 5·5 in) without a differential, and a streamlined body, shaped like a section from an aircraft wing, which completely enclosed the rear wheels.

Meanwhile, Gabriel Voisin had gone into production in 1921 with the C4, which had a four-cylinder engine of 60 × 110 mm (1244 cc) with two main bearings, developing 35 bhp. It had a track and wheelbase of 1·30 m (4 ft 3·2 in) ×

The 18 cv sleeve-valve Peugeots for the GP of Tours, 1923

The unit-construction engine and gearbox of the 18 cv Voisin: the first
version was called type M, perhaps because it was designed to the order
of André Citroën for Mors, before Voisin became interested, at a time
when Citroën still had Mors connections and hoped to rescue the
ancient make for a second time

Left: an impressive coupé-limousine on an 18 cv Peugeot, which left
the factory on 28th March 1924 (chassis number 35283)

The 18 cv Voisin, type M, in which the President of France went to the Grand Palais to open the 1921 Paris Motor Show

2·85 m (9 ft 4·2 in) and was endowed with four-wheel brakes in 1923. The little Voisin had its capacity raised to 1328 cc in 1924, by increasing the bore to 62 mm, when it was called C4S, and in 1925 it became C7, with a bigger bore enlargement to 67 mm (1552 cc) and a single disc clutch instead of a cone, though the three-speed gearbox was retained. The engine gave 44 bhp and two lengths of wheelbase were listed, 2·88 m (9 ft 5·4 in) and 2·98 m (9 ft 9·3 in).

Gabriel Voisin was always extremely interested in designing bodies of the greatest originality, both in shape and method of construction. First, he placed an aluminium floor, 5 to 7 mm thick, upon the chassis, where it was bolted down to the side members and spread outwards to the full width of the coachwork. The body was secured by its main members and had a wooden framework, panelled in sheet aluminium 3 mm thick. Voisin paid great attention to visibility, employing large windows which were inclined in order to reduce reflections; he also gave high priority to luggage space, which was arranged so that the carefully calculated weight distribution would not be upset.

Since 1910, Panhard had been building some models with Knight sleeve valves, alongside more numerous chassis with engines of classic design. In 1919, the great novelty was the 16 cv with sleeve valves, which had four cylinders, 85 × 140 mm (3178 cc), and a track of 1·38 m (4 ft 6·3 in), with a wheelbase of 2·84 m (9 ft 3·8 in) or 3·27 m (10 ft 0·9 in). This was soon followed by the 20 cv, also with sleeve valves, having four cylinders of 105 × 140 mm (4849 cc).

In 1922, Panhard discontinued production of all the old poppet-valve models, and introduce two new sleeve-valve engined chassis. The little X37 had a four-cylinder engine of 60 × 105 mm (1188 cc), a cone clutch and four-speed gearbox, and reversed quarter-elliptic rear springs like a Bugatti; it became X44 in 1924 when the bore was increased to 65 mm (1394 cc). The other new model in 1922 was the enormous 35 cv straight eight of 85 × 140 mm (6356 cc), with a track of 1·47 m (4 ft 9·9 in) and a wheelbase of 3·82 m (12 ft 6·4 in).

The 20 cv and the 35 cv were soon breaking speed records. As a matter of interest, in a 1921 road test of a 16 cv Sport, carried out by *La Vie Automobile,* the acceleration time from a standstill to 100 km/h (62 mph) was 11 seconds and the maximum speed 127 km/h (79 mph).

FOUR FROM THE AVIATION WORLD

Unveiled at the Paris Motor Show of 1919, the 32 cv Hispano-Suiza—called H6 and then H6B—was the star. It was the greatest, the French super-car, not by reason of its size or its cylinder capacity, for larger vehicles had been made, but for its technical superiority and all that it promised.

Its six-cylinder engine of 100 × 140 mm (6597 cc), which developed 120 bhp, was in fact half of a 12-cylinder aero engine. The cylinder block was in light alloy, the nitrided steel cylinder liners were screwed in, seven main bearings supported the crankshaft, and the valves were operated by an overhead camshaft, driven in front by a vertical shaft. There was dual ignition, with six sparking

Voisin: 18 cv coupé-limousine under construction

One of the first 18 cv Voisin limousines

An 18 cv Voisin for the GP of Strasbourg

A Voisin at Strasbourg

plugs on each side, the clutch was originally a cone but later a single disc, and the four-wheel brakes were assisted by a mechanical servo, driven from the three-speed gearbox. The car was capable of 130 km/h (81 mph) when fitted with a light body, but the Hispano often had to carry a heavy limousine or coupé de ville.

For lovers of speed, who were attracted to the Hispano, Marc Birkigt, the managing director as well as chief designer, produced, in 1924, the type H6C or 32 cv Sport, with cylinder dimensions of 110 × 140 mm (7983 cc) and an output of 140 bhp; the wheelbase was shortened to 3·39 m (11 ft 1·5 in), encouraging the use of light bodies, cabriolets and 'skiffs', those delightfully-named open torpedoes with boat-shaped tails. When the larger engine became available in a chassis with a 3·69 m (12 ft 1·3 in) wheelbase, it received the logical designation, corresponding to its fiscal rating, of 46 cv.

Hispano manufactured engines for aircraft, Farman made the fuselages. When the war was over, the Farman brothers turned towards the automobile and presented, in 1919, a

chassis of the same class as the Hispano, but which was never so successful. Perhaps this was due to its large and ungainly radiator, which discouraged coachbuilders from emulating the attractive bodies of its rival, but more likely it was because of certain mechanical shortcomings.

The engine, with six cylinders of 100 × 140 mm (6597 cc), had an overhead camshaft and a cylinder block of built-up construction, with welded sheet-steel water jackets. It had a cone clutch that was later replaced by multiple discs, with a four-speed, separately-mounted gearbox, and the cantilever rear springs were aided by a transverse spring. The Farman lacked the simplicity and the clean mechanical design of the Hispano and though it only developed 100 bhp, the makers claimed 140 km/h (87 mph) with an open torpedo body, though the weight was over two tons. First described as type A6A, it became A6B when unit construction of the engine and gearbox was adopted; the track was 1·42 m (4 ft 7·9 in) and the wheelbase 3·62 m (11 ft 10·5 in).

René Fonck was a fighter pilot and it was at the Brussels

The chassis of the C4 Voisin

A Voisin C4 saloon

Right: at the 1923 Paris Motor Show: a coachbuilt body by Maleval et Vacher in the purest cubist style

*René de Knyff's 16 cv sports Panhard with body by Labourdette:
timed at 127 km/h (79 mph)*

1920: a 12 cv poppet-valve Panhard-Levassor

Panhard-Levassor: a 20 cv touring car, type X29, of 1920

A 'skiff-cab' by Labourdette on one of the first 35 cv chassis, not yet fitted with front-wheel brakes

Panhard-Levassor: a coupé de ville on a 16 cv type X26 sleeve-valve
chassis

The gearbox and the brake-compensating cross shaft of the 10 cv Panhard-Levassor

Show of 1920 that he presented the car which was to carry his name. Like that of the Hispano, the radiator cap was embellished with a flying stork. The first Fonck was a car of medium size, with a four-cylinder engine of 80 × 130 mm (2614 cc). The overhead camshaft was driven by a vertical shaft, situated in the middle of the block and offset to the left of the crankshaft. The engine was in unit with a three-speed gearbox, there were no front brakes, and the track and wheelbase were 1·40 m (4 ft 7·1 in) and 3·10 m (10 ft 2 in).

At the Paris Show of 1921, Fonck exhibited a straight eight of which the engine had been shown separately at Brussels the previous year. With the same bore and stroke as the smaller model, its capacity was 5228 cc, and the general design was similar, with an overhead camshaft and three-speed gearbox—track 1·45 m (4 ft 9 in) and wheelbase 3·65 m (11 ft 11·7 in). The next year, a third model appeared, with six cylinders of identical bore and stroke giving 3921 cc and a track and wheelbase of 1·43 m (4 ft 8·3 in) × 3·50 m (11 ft 5·8 in) . . . but it is estimated that the total production of Fonck was only 10 to 12 cars.

Production of the Gnome-Rhône did not even reach these figures, for it was limited to a chassis and a saloon that appeared at the Paris Show of 1919. The six-cylinder, overhead camshaft engine had the generous dimensions of 115 × 140 mm (8725 cc), with a claimed output of 150 bhp, but after the Show the Gnome-Rhône faded into oblivion.

NOT FOR THE DILETTANTE

Among the manufacturers of quality cars with a medium production rate, from which all flights of fancy were absent, we should consider Ariès. The little 5 cv had dimensions of 60 × 80 mm (905 cc), the 10 cv of 70 × 120 mm (1847 cc) and the 15 cv was presented at the Paris Show of 1919 with an engine of 80 × 140 mm (2815 cc), of which the bore was increased around 1921–2 to 85 mm, giving 3178 cc. This last was available as a sports chassis, with a tuned engine and servo-assisted, four-wheel brakes.

Of rather dowdy appearance and a little on the heavy side, all these Ariès models hid four-cylinder, overhead-camshaft engines under their bonnets. With its cylinder bores reduced to 82 mm to bring it within the three-litre class, the 15 cv took part with success in many competitions up to 1930.

The Chenard-Walcker was equally, between the two wars, what most people would call a serious car; its greatest period was 1923–7, as a result of numerous racing successes. In 1921, the range consisted of three four-cylinder chassis: the 10 cv, 70 × 130 mm (2001 cc), the 12 cv, 75 × 150 mm (2651 cc), and the 15/18 cv, 80 × 150 mm (3016 cc).

A three-litre Sport, with a 90 bhp engine having inclined valves in hemispherical combustion chambers, operated by a shaft-driven overhead camshaft, won the first 24 Hour race at Le Mans at an average of 92 km/h (57 mph), in 1923. After this, Chenard created a two-litre of 70 × 130 mm, of similar technical design, then a twin-carburettor straight-eight of the same bore and stroke, developing 130 bhp, which ran at Le Mans in 1924, breaking the lap record at 116 km/h (72 mph). In its original form, the straight-eight resembled the three-litre, but it was redesigned and lowered for 1925, when it won the 24 Hours race at Spa.

Right: a 1922 Panhard advertisement

'Retromobile' exhibition 1975: a 1922 Hispano 32 cv skiff

Farman: the well-streamlined sports-torpedo of the famous airman, Nungesser

Hurtu had only a
small production but they were just as
serious, though they did little to make people talk about their
cars. Established before 1900 and making sewing machines as
well as automobiles, in 1923 the firm of Hurtu started
production, alongside their traditional 12/14 cv, of a new
two-litre car of the popular 70 × 130 mm dimensions. It had
overhead valves in a detachable head and the crankshaft was
on three main bearings, with a single-disc clutch, a four-
speed gearbox, and four-wheel brakes.

Among these honest cars, let us mention Le Zèbre, designed
and manufactured by the celebrated engineer Salomon, who
created little single-cylinder cars before 1914 and was later to
be responsible for the first 10 cv Citroën. Le Zèbre built a
small four-cylinder model in 1920, of 55 × 105 mm (998 cc),
followed in 1924 by a larger four-cylinder car of 69 ×
132 mm (1974 cc). Though the engine had side valves, it had

Farman: a special body designed for performances that were never achieved

Right: 'A car runs, the Farman glides' (1924 advertisement)

90

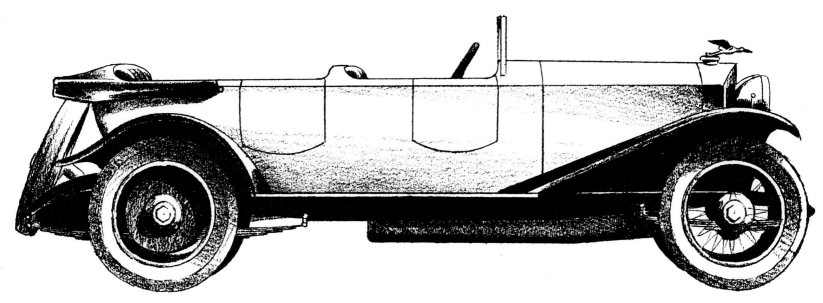

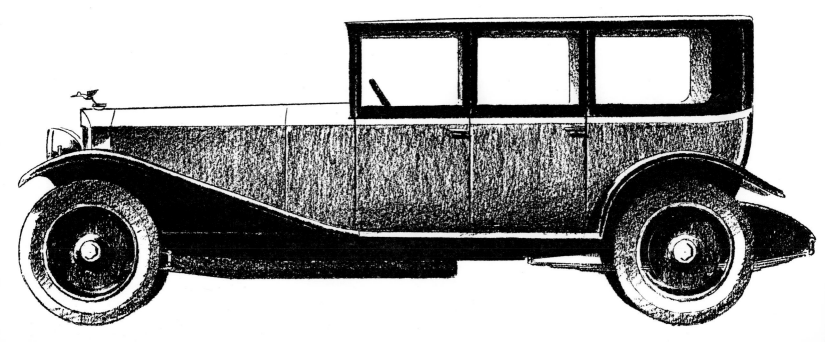

a turbulent cylinder head designed on Sir Harry Ricardo's principles.

ADVANCED TECHNIQUES

The two-litre Sizaire Frères, which was presented at the Paris Show of 1923, was the successor of the Sizaire et Naudin that had independent front suspension, and was itself the first French car with independent suspension of all four wheels. The system was complicated but, in its essentials, it consisted of lower transverse leaf springs and upper wishbones, front and rear, with the differential unit mounted on the chassis. The four-cylinder, overhead-camshaft engine had dimensions of 76 × 110 mm (1996 cc) and there was a sports version with sixteen valves, while a supercharger was used in a few cases.

THE MARGINAL MAKES

These were numerous. Some builders, like Claude Delage, were happy to use Ballot engines and chassis of classical architecture, often obtained complete from a specialist tradesman. It was easy, in the period under review, to construct a car, buying proprietary bits—engine, clutch, gearbox, chassis, steering, brakes—from outside suppliers. It was only necessary to assemble them . . . and to choose a radiator to give the make its personality.

Other small manufacturers attempted to break new ground, without going as far as Sizaire—though perhaps some went too far, nevertheless. Among them were De Bazelaire, with a chassis-mounted differential and articulated drive shafts, and Gobron, who left the straight and narrow in pursuit of opposed-piston engines.

Wattel-Mortier presented, around 1921, an engine without poppet valves differing completely from the Knight—it had six cylinders of 70 × 115 mm (2655 cc). Each cylinder had beside it a piston valve, as on a steam locomotive, which uncovered ports communicating with the combustion chambers during the inlet and exhaust strokes. The upward movements were secured by a camshaft and the valves were

1923: the engine of the 5 cv Ariès. The dog for the starting handle is on the front of the overhead camshaft

returned by springs. The constructor claimed greater simplicity than the sleeve valves of Knight or Burt McCullum could offer.

Octo created a car, using the Ballot engine, which had a progressive eight-speed transmission, built under Domecq-Cazaux patents. An Octo advertisement tells us that 'the idea is as follows: to retain for the chassis the conventional layout normally adopted, but to substitute for the gearbox a simple, flexible, and silent mechanism, permitting an extended range of speeds to be changed without fumbling or noise . . . The clutch and gearbox are combined in one simple device provided with two friction linings . . . in the positions giving reduced speed or reverse, the first lining works by friction against the engine flywheel under favourable operating conditions never attained by the old arrangement of discs at 90° . . . in the high speed position, the first lining is not used, the clutch by direct cone is obtained by means of the second lining, etc.' All that scarcely seems very serious and it is difficult to say whether any Octos really motored or not.

The small manufacturers were not all impractical visionaries, even though they did try some original solutions.

ARIÈS

VOITURES DE TOURISME
5 - 10 - 15 HP

VÉHICULES INDUSTRIELS
pour toutes applications
(CHARGES UTILES 500 à 5.000 KILOS)

....

DIRECTION COMMERCIALE:
27, Avenue .Marceau — COURBEVOIE (Seine)
Tél.: WAGRAM 82-50, 82-94

USINES A
COURBEVOIE — PARIS — VILLENEUVE-LA-GARENNE (Seine)

LA NOUVELLE **15** HP **ARIÈS**

— MODÈLE 1922 —

SORT ACTUELLEMENT EN SÉRIE.

Construite avec la même précision qu'un moteur d'aviation, avec la même robustesse qu'un camion

Moteur 4 cylindres 85×140 ; allumage jumelé.
Embrayage à disques métalliques.
Boîte à 4 vitesses et marche arrière.

Double réservoir d'essence ; exhausteur.
Éclairage et démarrage électriques.
Roues tôle, amovibles ; pneus de 880×120.

Adresser toutes demandes au Siège Social : 63, AVENUE DES CHAMPS-ÉLYSÉES, PARIS

Téléphone : PASSY 87-90, 87-94

Métro : MARBEUF

USINES A

COURBEVOIE, 27, Avenue Marceau. Téléphone { WAG. 82-50 } » 82-94

PARIS, VILLENEUVE-LA-GARENNE (Seine)

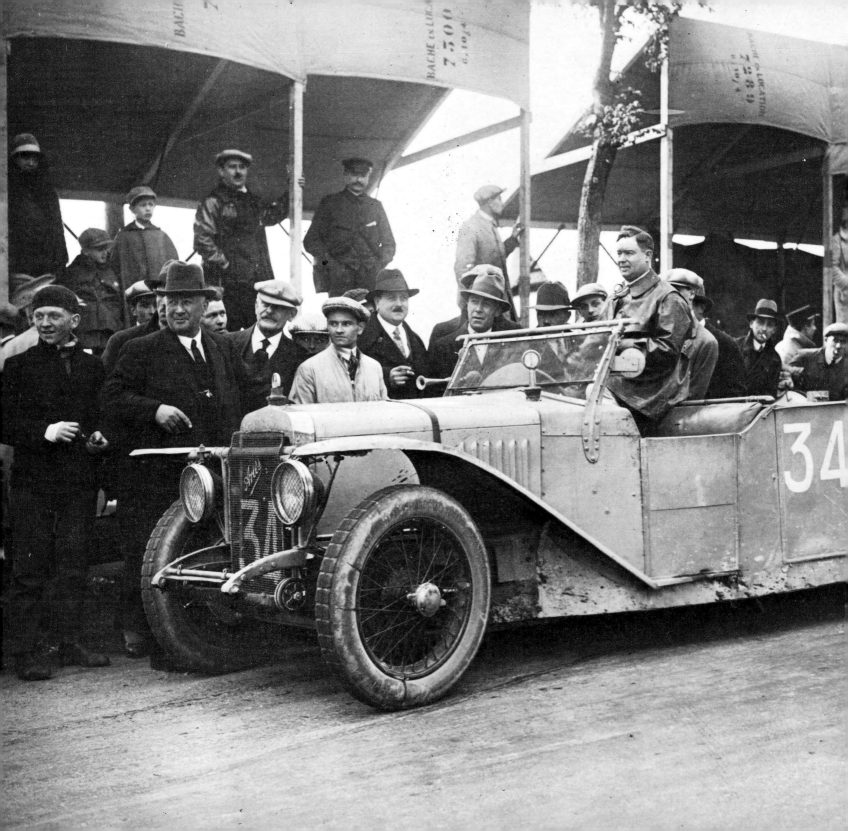

Thus, the SARA was the first French car, apart from cyclecars, with air cooling. It had a four-cylinder engine with pushrod-operated overhead valves, with dimensions of 62 × 91 mm (1099 cc). The separate cylinder barrels were well-finned and supplied with air through aluminium ducts from a centrifugal blower running on ball bearings. The blower, it was claimed, used only 3 bhp, that is to say less than an ordinary fan. Some SARAs acquitted themselves well in endurance events, such as the Le Mans 24 Hour race.

Finally, one must recognize that some of these small manufacturers, far from seeking originality at any price or, at least, new formulae, were accustomed to maintaining a balance between classicism and futuristic techniques. We should be grateful to them for some interesting designs and regret that they did not catch on. Majola, a pioneer of overhead camshafts and ball-bearing crankshafts, was a make which deserved greater recognition and a happier fate. The Alva-Sport, in 1921, had a four-cylinder engine of 75 × 130 mm (2297 cc), with three main bearings and pushrod-operated overhead valves. If the clutch was still a cone, the gearbox had four speeds and there was a four-wheel braking system.

As for the Oméga-Six, it was designed by engineer Gadoux (ex-Hispano) and built by the Etablissements Daubec; it was certainly a car of the front rank in 1922. It had six cylinders of 65 × 100 mm (1991 cc), with a single overhead camshaft driven by a vertical shaft and bevel gears, the power output being 55 bhp. The brakes were on all four wheels and though a cone clutch and a three-speed gearbox were used, the later three-litre model was more advanced in these respects.

Left: the three-litre Ariès in its lowered form—it was nicknamed 'the Bug'

Targa Florio 1923: a Chenard in action. This make won the very first 24 Hour race at Le Mans

The straight-eight Chenard-Walcker of 1925

Right: Chenard et Walcker, a 1924 advertisement

SOCIÉTÉ ANONYME
DES ANCIENS ETABLISSEMENTS

CHENARD
&
WALCKER

GENNEVILLIERS (SEINE)

The straightforward, unpretentious 10 cv Hurtu

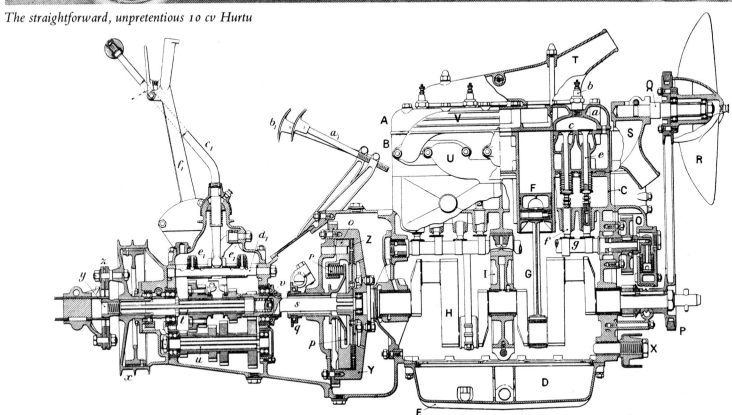

The engine of the last Zèbre and its Ricardo cylinder head

An original sports torpedo on a Sizaire Frères chassis

The chassis of the De Bazelaire with its chassis-mounted differential and articulated driveshafts

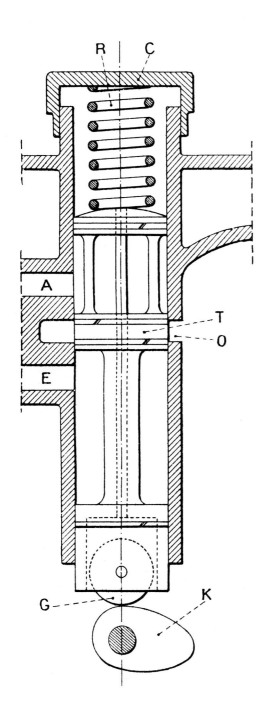

Section of the Wattel-Mortier piston valve

Two views of the SARA chassis, showing the tubular front axle and transverse spring as well as the centrifugal blower for cooling

The Octo chassis, showing the peculiar transmission

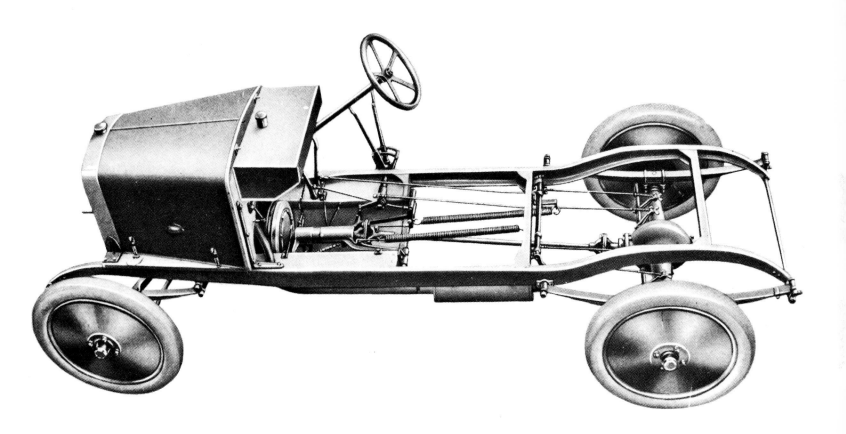

The front of the SARA in the Le Mans museum

1921: the front of the Alva Sport, worthy of a chassis of 1930

Oméga-Six: the chassis

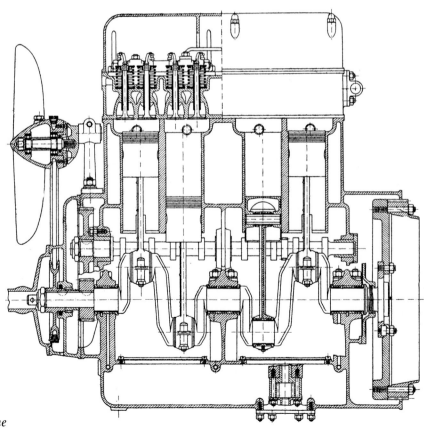

Section of the Alva Sport engine

The front of the Oméga-Six

The Oméga-Six engine of 1922

The Oméga-Six as seen by an advertising artist

The Provincials

Up to the beginning of the 1930s, if not until the last war, Parisians were inclined to regard provincials with some condescension and, conversely, those sturdy folk prided themselves on their common sense, compared with the whims and pretensions of the inhabitants of the capital.

This was true of men, and equally so of cars. There was a tendency, in Paris, to be scornful of the cars manufactured in the provinces, especially when most of their sales were local, and to think that the best and most famous makes were inevitably Parisian.

Whether one likes it or not, while it is perfectly true that certain cars built in the provinces were of peasant stock, it is equally correct that some from Paris were just as rustic, as we shall see; we shall also get to know some provincial makes that, for technical excellence, had no need to envy Parisian productions. Let us not forget that Lyons, Sochaux, and Nantes—and especially Molsheim—are not precisely at the gates of Paris.

PEUGEOT

The Peugeot family originated at Doubs, remaining there for many generations. Peugeot cars were built around Montbeliard, at Beaulieu, at Audincourt, at Velentigney, and at Sochaux, amongst a tough community that respected substantial and accurate work which was well done. This was the background from which the cars were produced, often designed without great imagination but invariably built with excellent workmanship—cars on which one could always depend.

Leaving out the sleeve-valve models and the baby Quadrilette, these cars, all with four cylinders, were:

—type 159 68 × 100 mm (1453 cc);

—type 153B 82 × 130 mm (2746 cc), later 85 × 130 mm (2951 cc), from which were developed types 153BR, 153BRA, 153 BRS Sport, with pushrod-operated overhead valves, 153C, and 153CA, colonial;

—series 163, including types 163 and 163B 66 × 105 mm (1437 cc), types 163BR, 163BRS, 163 BS 67 × 105 mm (1481 cc);

—type 173S 68 × 105 mm (1525 cc), pushrods;

—type 175 85 × 130 mm (2951 cc), pushrods:

—the long series 177, beginning in 1923 with 177B 68 × 105 mm (1525 cc), detachable cylinder head.

Except where indicated, these all had side-valve engines with non-detachable heads, multiple disc clutches, four-speed gearboxes, and rear-wheel brakes only. The worm-drive rear axle first appeared on the 153.

In 1924, Peugeot replaced the indestructible but uncomfortable Quadrilette by the 5 cv, which retained the same mechanism, a four-cylinder engine 50 × 85 mm (668 cc), developing 11 bhp, and a combined gearbox and rear axle, without a differential. It was distinguished from its predecessor by a large choice of bodies and by a serious increase in weight from 350 kg (770 lb) to 520 kg (1144 lb).

An 11 cv Donnet-Zedel

SWISS CARS IN FRANCE

Not far from Sochaux, at Pontarlier, the Société Zedel manufactured, from 1906 onwards, some robust cars. Zedel, or ZL, was a make started in France by two Swiss, Zurcher and Luthi, who had made motor-cycles and various accessories, such as sparking plugs, in their native land. After 1914, the Zedel range consisted of a big four-cylinder car, 85 × 140 mm (3178 cc), and the type C16, another four-cylinder model and quite modern for its date, 75 × 120 mm (2121 cc), with a side-valve engine, detachable cylinder head,

a four-speed gearbox, and optional front brakes.

At the end of 1923, Jérôme Donnet, a Swiss who had been a hotelier, a car dealer, and an aircraft manufacturer, bought the Pontarlier factory, where the new firm of Donnet-Zedel continued production of the C16. Towards the end of 1924, the celebrated Swiss engineer, Ernest Henry, who created the fabulous racing Peugeots before 1914, designed a little Donnet-Zedel called type G, 62 × 91 mm (1099 cc). This new car was built at Nanterre, in a factory which Donnet had just bought from Vinot-Deguingand, and

A Franco-Swiss car, the 'Pic-Pic' (Piccard-Pictet)

which Simca took over ten years later before letting it go to Citroën.

Piccard-Pictet, another Swiss manufacturer, built good cars at home and in France simultaneously, which were familiarly called 'Pic-Pic'. They had sleeve-valve engines, built under Burt McCullum patents, with single sleeves having a combined vertical and rotary motion, as opposed to the Knight system with double sleeves moving vertically only. The first post-war Pic-Pic was a four-cylinder 16 cv, 85 ×

130 mm (2951 cc), which was sold in normal and sports versions.

RENAULTS AT BESANÇON?

At Besançon in 1920, Théophile Schneider abandoned the Renault-style bonnet to which he had been faithful and, ten years before Billancourt, adopted the front radiator. His production at that time consisted of a 12 cv, four cylinders 75 × 130 mm (2297 cc), a 14 cv, also four cylinders 82·5 × 140 mm (3030 cc), an 18/20 cv, with six cylinders of the same

The very clean design of the 11/12 cv Vermorel engine

A 1922 10/12 cv Vermorel touring car

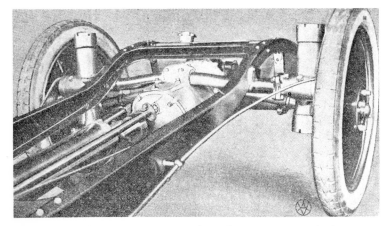

Beck, 1921: the rear suspension. The coil springs are inside the cylindrical housings that also act as shock absorbers

bore and stroke (4545 cc), and a 26 cv, four cylinders 96 × 190 mm—yes 190 mm, you read it right—(5501 cc), resurrecting a pre-war technique. Théo-Schneiders normally had side valves, but overhead-valve cylinder heads were offered at extra cost. In 1925 a two-litre car, four cylinders 72 × 120 mm, was introduced, of more modern design. It was to remain in production for nearly ten years, but the sales of the Théo-Schneiders were always limited to the region where they were made.

THE LYONS MOTOR-CARS

These formed by far the most important group of provincials, both for the number of manufacturers and their total production, at least during the years we are considering.

The Vermorel—sturdy, utilitarian, and reliable—resembled without doubt the provincial woman lacking grace and charm, just as one might imagine. Three chassis were in production at the beginning of the twenties, all with unit construction of the four-cylinder engine and gearbox but also with a leather cone clutch and side valves; all three gave an impression of seriousness and boredom. They were the 12/16 cv of 1921, 74 × 130 mm (2236 cc), the 10 cv of 1922, 70 × 110 mm (1693 cc), and the 15 cv, also of 1922, 80 × 130 mm (2614 cc). The track and wheelbase dimensions were 1·30 m (4 ft 3·2 in) × 2·90 m (9 ft 6·2 in) for the 10 cv and 1·40 m (4 ft 7·1 in) × 3·10 m (10 ft 2 in) for the 12/16 and 15 cv, these chassis being fitted either with rather old-fashioned coachwork or bodies for commercial purposes.

L'ASS (Automobiles Sans Soupapes—cars without valves) was a firm which offered, very briefly, a two-cylinder two-stroke car of 1200 cc.

At the Brussels Motor Show of 1921, Beck exhibited the prototype of a car with independent suspension of all four wheels. The differential assembly was mounted on a tubular cross-member that carried vertical cylinders on its ends, containing coil springs and full of glycerine for hydraulic damping, which formed the suspension medium for the rear

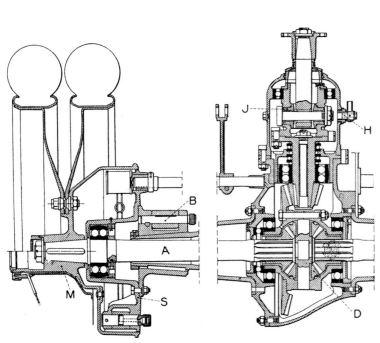

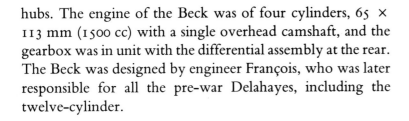

Cottin-Desgouttes 18 cv 1921: the rear axle and twin wheels

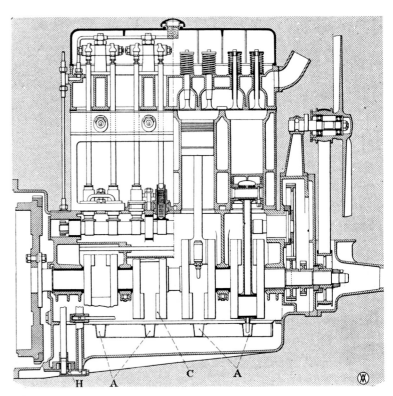

The 1922 12 cv Cottin-Desgouttes engine

hubs. The engine of the Beck was of four cylinders, 65 × 113 mm (1500 cc) with a single overhead camshaft, and the gearbox was in unit with the differential assembly at the rear. The Beck was designed by engineer François, who was later responsible for all the pre-war Delahayes, including the twelve-cylinder.

The Barron-Vialle was a creation of engineer Gadoux around 1923, after much experimental work with prototypes, which were largely constructed of Alpax light alloy. Among these was a six-cylinder car of 70 × 90 mm (2078 cc), with a single overhead camshaft, and an eight-cylinder model of 2750 cc.

Cognet-de-Seynes restarted the production in 1920 of a little 6 cv car with a four-cylinder engine, 57 × 110 mm (1123 cc),

which dated from 1913 but was of a somewhat remarkable architecture. The engine, clutch, gearbox, and back axle were rigidly assembled in a single unit, attached to the chassis by a knee-joint situated between the flywheel and the crankcase. The whole outfit oscillated about this joint when the springs deflected and naturally there was no need for any universal joints.

Berliet became world famous in 1908 by selling to ALCO, an American firm specializing largely in railway equipment, the licence to manufacture one of their chassis. That is the origin of the locomotive which appears on the Berliet badge. In 1916, by an inverse movement—but this time without any sort of licence—Berliet had copied the Dodge, line for line. The French car, built of inferior metals, was a disaster and the type VB, for so it was called, was hastily replaced by the VL, a

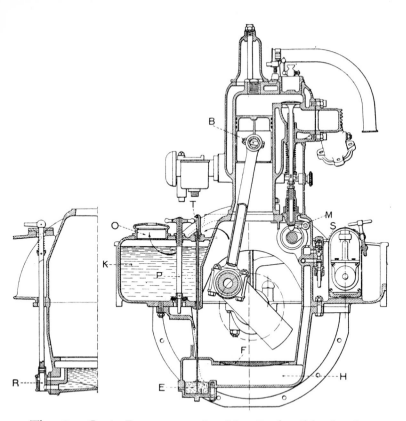

The 18 cv Cottin-Desgouttes engine. Note R, the oil level and drainage tap, E, the float of the gauge, K, the reserve oil tank, and M, a cam follower operating an adjustable tappet

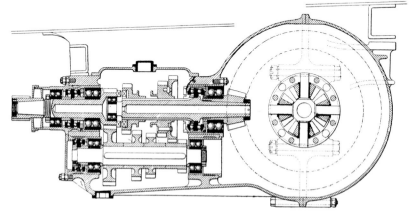

The combined gearbox and final drive of the SLIM

new 16 cv four-cylinder car that was also named the Silver Star, with dimensions of 90 × 130 mm (3308 cc). The VF, with four cylinders of 80 × 130 mm (2614 cc), was virtually the VB with a 12 cv engine instead of its former 15 cv unit, and a smattering of the VL here and there. The range was completed by a big 22 cv machine, also with four cylinders, of 100 × 140 mm (4398 cc). These years were far from glorious for the old firm of Lyons.

Another Lyons make enjoyed great local renown, supported by some success in hillclimbs, such as Limonest, Planfoy, les Alpilles, Laffrey, and La Faucille. It was La Buire (after the place de la Buire, at Lyons), of which the 10 cv of 1923–4 cut

off the grizzled hair of the preceding models. Its monobloc engine had four cylinders of 70 × 120 mm (1847 cc) and three main bearings, the clutch was of the multiple disc type, the gearbox had four speeds, and four-wheel brakes were standard.

More interesting, technically, was the Cottin-Desgouttes. A new 18 cv four-litre chassis was presented at the Lyons Fair of 1919, beside the old models of 14, 23, and 32 cv. In October 1922, a truly modern car appeared, a four-cylinder 12 cv, 80 × 130 mm (2614 cc), with five main crankshaft bearings, pushrod-operated overhead valves, and four-wheel brakes. In 1923, Cottin-Desgouttes presented a six-cylinder car of the same bore and stroke with a seven-bearing crankshaft.

There followed a sports three-litre prototype, with four cylinders of 83 × 138 mm (2987 cc), three valves per

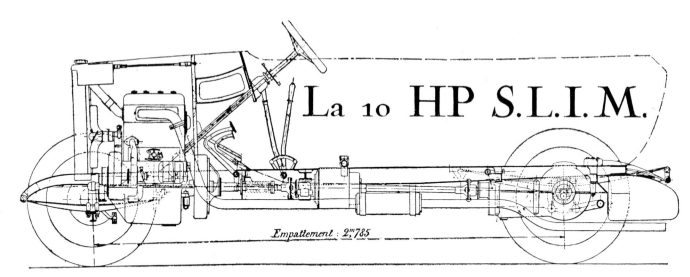

Side elevation of the SLIM chassis

cylinder, two carburettors, and dual ignition. From this, three cars were developed which were entered for the touring category of the Grand Prix of the ACF, and they carried off the first two places. The bore and stroke had been reduced to 80 × 132 mm (2654 cc), there was only one carburettor, and this time four valves per cylinder were employed. A production version was called type MS3 or GP 3 litres. Later Cottin-Desgouttes was to produce an interesting series of cars with independent suspension of all four wheels, called the 'Sans-Secousses' ('No Jolt').

The SLIM (of which few were made) was a skilful mixture of obsolescent practice with original ideas. The engine, with four cylinders of 65 × 130 mm (1726 cc), had 16 valves, operated by pushrods and rockers from two camshafts in the crank-case, and while the cylinder head was detachable, the water circulation did not pass through the gasket. The gearbox was in unit with the differential and was

mounted on the chassis, with rear suspension by a De Dion axle on three-quarter elliptic springs. The two-piece propeller shaft was bisected by the starter motor, which carried universal joints at both ends. It was alleged that the car would move off very smoothly on the starter alone, the engine subsequently being brought into action by engaging the clutch.

Rochet Schneider, who built 'the car of quality', also claimed to offer 'Strength, Simplicity, Silence'. These assertions were true without any doubt, in 1922, of the 12 cv, four cylinders 80 × 130 mm (2614 cc), of the 18 cv, 95 × 140 mm (3969 cc), and of the big six-cylinder car, 100 × 130 mm (6126 cc). However, these heavy chassis, on which one could certainly rely implicitly under all circumstances, inspired thoughts of Delaunay-Belleville and of other cars that were out of date by the length of the war. After 1923, Rochet-Schneiders were modernized and fitted with overhead valve

The 15/25 cv Turcat-Méry chassis, a provincial of conservative but well-considered design

Rochet-Schneider, 1921. From a very good family but lacking in elegance and style

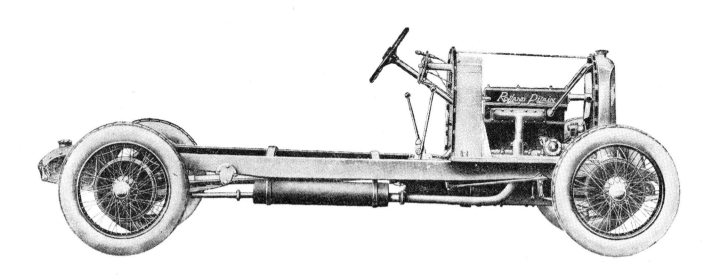

1924, the two-litre Rolland-Pilain chassis. This provincial has no need to be envious of Paris

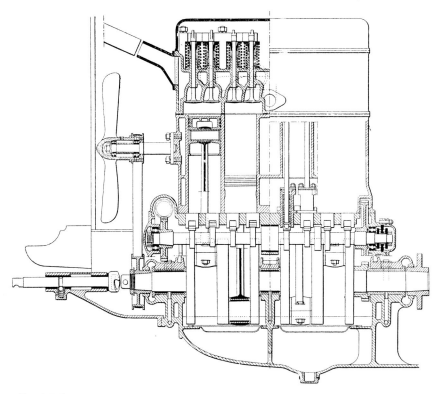

The engine of the 12 cv sports Rolland-Pilain

Rolland-Pilain: hydraulic front brake

engines, when they deserved to be classed among the most
beautiful cars of France.

THE MARSEILLAISES

Turcat-Méry started manufacturing cars in 1896 and sold a
licence to De Dietrich to build one of their models in 1902.
Three years later, the Societé Lorraine des Anciens Etablissements De Dietrich took control of the Marseilles firm and
produced both Lorraine-Dietrich and Turcat-Méry cars up
to 1914. After the war, a new Turcat-Méry firm, independent of Lorraine, was founded but went into liquidation
almost immediately. Yet another Turcat-Méry company
was set up in 1924, which finally ceased activities at the
beginning of the 30s.

At the Paris Show of 1921, Turcat-Méry presented a
'new' 15/25 cv chassis, with four cylinders of 80 × 150 mm
(3016 cc), Although it was new, the type PG, with its track
and wheelbase of 1·45 m (4 ft 9 in) × 3·28 m (10 ft 9·1 in),

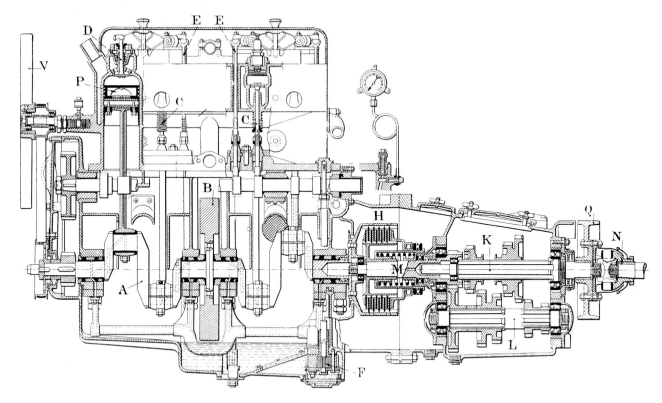

Section of the Motobloc engine. Note the flywheel in the middle of the crankshaft

Georges Roy. A few small changes, such as wire wheels, could make this a handsome car

Motobloc was the first manufacturer to build up the engine, clutch, and gearbox as one unit. This is the 15 cv engine with inlet-over-exhaust valves

The Léon Laisne suspension in its later form

revived the techniques of long ago and its heavy and ageing character was accentuated by the bodies with which it was tarted up—and that expression has never been so thoroughly deserved.

Technically more seductive than her neighbour, the Paulet nevertheless had a short life and much smaller production figures than the Turcat-Méry. However, here is the advanced specification: six cylinders, 75 × 130 mm (3446 cc) in 1922, 80 × 130 mm (3921 cc) in 1923, a single overhead camshaft driven by bevel gears and a vertical shaft, seven main bearings, unit construction, multiple disc clutch, and four-wheel brakes; the track and wheelbase were 1·42 m (4 ft 7·9 in) and 3·25 m (10 ft 8 in) or 3·50 m (11 ft 5·8 in).

TOURS: THE ROLLAND-PILAINS

If one were only going to recognize a single virtue in Rolland-Pilain, the manufacturer from Tours, it would be that of having fitted hydraulic brakes to production cars—and not just prototypes—since 1920. To be precise, the hydraulic brakes were only on the front wheels, the same pedal retarding the rear wheels through a transmission brake on the back of the gearbox, a hand lever operating shoes mechanically in the rear drums. The Rolland-Pilains of the twenties were agreeable touring cars, well designed and of pleasing appearance. These remarks apply to the 10 cv, with four cylinders of 70 × 125 mm (1924 cc), called type RP2 in 1919, RP in 1920; to the 18 cv, four cylinders 95 × 140 mm (3969 cc), types CR2 and CR; and to the 14 cv type M6 or, above all, to the 12 cv, 74 × 130 mm (2236 cc) and 75 × 130 mm (2297 cc), which was offered in standard form with side valves or as an overhead-valve sports car.

FROM TOURS TO BORDEAUX

The Georges Roy was among those provincial makes, of which neither the sales nor the reputation extended outside the area where they were made, and nothing about the design offered the least excuse for excitement. The 14 cv, which the Bordeaux firm built in the early twenties, had a four-cylinder side-valve engine of 85 × 130 mm (2951 cc) with a non-detachable cylinder head, which was mounted on a sub-frame, along with the separate gearbox, and there were no front brakes. The bodies for these chassis were also built in the Georges Roy factory, without any sign of imagination.

However, there was some nice detail work among the mechanical parts. The tappets were adjustable, the fan ran on ball bearings and the tension of its belt was set with a wing nut, while small coil springs beneath the leather of the male cone gave the clutch a progressive engagement. Although the Georges Roy was of sound construction, it seemed a good deal lighter than many cars of similar conception, and it was built with the craftsmanship that characterized most chassis of provincial origin.

Common sense presided also at the creation of the Motobloc, which owed its name to the fact that, ever since 1905, the cars produced by this second Bordeaux manufacturer had the engine, clutch, and gearbox built up as one unit. But this, which was considered highly original at that epoch, was not the only unusual characteristic of Motoblocs. To obtain better balance and reduce crankshaft fatigue, the flywheel was placed in the middle of the engine—which incidentally gave a four-bearing crankshaft for four cylinders—and as the multiple-disc clutch was enclosed in an oil-tight case, the gearbox could share the oil in the crank-case. The final affectation was that the valve gear was of the inlet-over-exhaust type, with pushrod-operated inlets and side exhaust valves.

The Motobloc range between 1920 and 1925 was composed of the following four-cylinder cars: type S, 65 × 100 mm (1327 cc), track 1·20 m (3 ft 11·2 in) and wheelbase 2·50 m (8 ft 2·4 in); type R, 70 × 110 mm (1693 cc) later 65 × 110 mm (1460 cc), track 1·30 m (4 ft 3·2 in) and wheelbase 3·00 m (9 ft 10·1 in), type O, 74 × 120 mm (2064 cc), track 1·30 m (4 ft 3·2 in) and wheelbase 3·10 m (10 ft 2 in); type OB, 80 × 120 mm (2413 cc), track 1·35 m (4 ft 5·1 in) and wheelbase 3·33 m (10 ft 11·1 in); type OD, 80 × 148 mm (2976 cc), track 1·40 m (4 ft 7·1 in) and wheelbase 3·30 m (10 ft 9·9 in).

FROM NANTES . . .

Born in 1880, Léon Laisne built his first car at the age of 19; fitter, turner, and inventor, he designed chassis well before 1914 that were fitted with lever-type suspension. Installed in a workshop at Nantes, he made machine tools and shells from 1916 and after the war he changed back to automobile engineering, putting his first model on the market in 1919. Type A had a Ballot engine with four cylinders of 75 × 130 mm (2297 cc) and was characterized by its highly original independent suspension of all four wheels, in which levers carrying the stub-axles acted against coil springs in vertical tubes fixed to the chassis. Type A was followed by type B, with detail improvements, then type D of 70 × 120 mm (1847 cc), and type F, with a SCAP engine of 70 × 110 mm (1693 cc) and four-wheel brakes. Two very small cars were also built, type E of 55 × 84 mm (798 cc) and type H of 61 × 105 mm (1227 cc).

Serge Pozzoli has told me that a competition prototype existed, type C, created for the Grand Prix des Voiturettes at Le Mans in 1920, in which the cylinders containing the springs were placed horizontally. This location was afterwards adopted for production models.

. . . TO LE MANS

Starting in 1842 as bell founders and soon well known as competent engineers, the Bollées attacked the problem of vehicles driven by steam in 1873 and they must be regarded as the pioneers of automobile locomotion. Their first petrol-engined machine was a tricycle of 1895, followed by a four-wheeler in 1900. During the period 1919–22, the Léon Bollée range included: type M1, later P, 12 cv four cylinders 80 × 130 mm (2614 cc); type M2, 15 cv four cylinders 85 × 130 mm (2951 cc); type M3, four cylinders 95 × 130 mm (3686 cc); type G, 18 cv six cylinders 83 × 110 mm (3571 cc); and type N, 20 cv six cylinders 80 × 130 mm (3921 cc).

For 1923, type P stayed in production, alone of the existing range. Two new models were added, a 10 cv with pushrod-operated valves in a detachable head, 72 × 120 mm

(1954 cc), and a 20 cv with six cylinders and an overhead camshaft. These two new chassis, unlike their predecessors, had multiple disc clutches and four-wheel brakes.

AND AT ORLEANS

At Orléans, in a factory which Panhard were to buy around 1930 for building their coachwork, the firm of Delaugère et Clayette produced, early in the twenties, cars with both sleeve and poppet valves which built up a nice little reputation for themselves. There were two four-cylinder

models, type AX, 10/12 cv 70 × 140 mm (2155 cc), and type AY, 14/16 cv 85 × 140 mm (3178 cc). The six-cylinder model was type 6Z, 18/22 cv 85 × 140 mm (4767 cc).

IN THE NORTH

The periods immediately before and just after the first world war saw the birth of an incredible number of tiny manufacturers, who assembled cars of which nothing was original except the shape of their radiators. Their workshops might equally well be in Paris, including its suburbs such as Levallois, Asnières, and Courbevoie, or in the provinces, but they made none of the principal components themselves, obtaining them 'outside' from specialist manufacturers. Among these were Ballot, Ruby, CIME, SCAP, and Chapuis-Dornier for engines, Malicet et Blin for gearboxes, Lemaître et Gérard for axles, Perrot for brakes, of which a suitable selection was mounted on a chassis by Paquis or Arbel.

The firm of Paquis made chassis at a factory in the Ardennes, which were bought by many of the smaller constructors, but they also had a subsidiary workshop in a Paris suburb, where they built the engines for Salomon's Zèbres. In 1919, the directors of Paquis decided to sell complete chassis with Ballot engines under their own trade mark, SUP (Societé des Usines du Paquis), and several hundred such vehicles were produced. Subsequently, the SUP factories concentrated on the manufacture of the Hinstin cyclecar.

The Guilick, made at Maubeuge, might almost be regarded as a SUP with a different radiator badge, and was a typical example of a small provincial make. It was completely unknown in Paris but the 11 cv Guilick was exhibited several times at the Brussels Show, fitted with the inevitable Ballot engine of 66 × 130 mm (1779 cc).

Another example was the Delfosse, which was also manufactured in the north of France, at Cambrai, and took on a sporting character as it developed. The make began in 1922 as a very small car, fitted with a Morain-Sylvestre twin-cylinder engine with a capacity of about one litre, which was soon replaced by a side-valve four-cylinder Chapuis-Dornier of 60 × 85 mm (961 cc). The production of both versions of this model did not exceed twenty cars. After that, Delfosse used the four-cylinder CIME engine in various sizes, such as 62 × 91 mm (1099 cc), 64 × 93·5 mm (1203 cc), and 68 × 103 mm (1496 cc). The Delfosse had an original rear suspension system. Reversed quarter-elliptic springs, Bugatti-style, were used, but instead of being rigidly

Bugatti: the type 22 in the museum of Bec-Hellouin

mounted they were on trunnions which could turn on the tubular rear crossmember. The turning movement was resisted by another pair of quarter-elliptic springs, also bolted to the trunnions by their thick ends but facing forward, their other ends being attached to the chassis by shackles, just ahead of the axle. This suspension was claimed to have a self-damping effect and there were also built-in friction-type dampers, oscillating on the same axis as the springs.

ALSACE REGAINED

At Strasbourg, Mathis, having become a Frenchman by the victory over Germany, went back into production in 1919 with his pre-war types PB and PC. In 1921, he was building the type S 6/8 cv, with four cylinders of 58 × 100 mm (1057 cc), a leather cone clutch and three-speed gearbox; it had a track of 1·05 m (3 ft 5·3 in) and a wheelbase of 2·30 m

*All about the
10 cv Mathis*

A Bugatti type 30 today

(7 ft 6·5 in). From this the type SB 8/10 cv was developed, with dimensions of 60 × 100 mm (1131 cc), a multiple disc clutch and a four-speed gearbox; there were three alternative wheelbase lengths, type SB 2·40 m (7 ft 10·5 in), type SBA 2·60 m (8 ft 6·4 in), and type SBL 2·85 m (9 ft 4·2 in). A later version of the SB had pushrod-operated overhead valves.

Entirely new was the 6 cv of 55 × 90 mm (855 cc), which was intended to compete with the 5 cv Citroën. It had unit construction and a three-bearing crankshaft, with a multiple-disc clutch and a four-speed gearbox, but the cylinder head was non-detachable.

Bugatti . . . one seeks in vain for a definition: the most Italian of the French cars, the Italian car which was all but German and became French, the provincial that was right at the top, ahead of all the Parisians—is it not simply a Bugatti, an Ettore Bugatti? Whatever it may be, the post-war period brought

us types 22 and 23, with four-cylinder, 16-valve engines, and a three-litre prototype. This was the first eight-cylinder Bugatti touring car and it was notable for a certain number of original features, such as a two-speed gearbox in unit with the rear axle, twin front springs, duplicated track rod and drag link, rear shock absorbers concealed within the brake drums, and an adjustable steering wheel with two spokes close together.

The first production eight-cylinder Bugatti touring car was the type 30, of which the engine was very similar to those used in the Grand Prix at Strasbourg. The dimensions were 60 × 88 mm (1991 cc), with three valves per cylinder, and the wheelbase was retained at 2·85 mm (9 ft 4·2 in) after a few early examples of 2·40 m (7 ft 10·5 in) and 2·55 m (8 ft 4·4 in). Early cars had hydraulic operation of the front brakes and cables to the rear, but later all the brakes had mechanical operation by cables.

Mass Production

When André Citroën proclaimed, at the beginning of 1919, that he was about to begin the manufacture of cars by mass production, nobody took him seriously. Some thought that he would never reach the stage where vehicles were actually rolling off the production lines, while others believed that he would get that far, followed by the inevitable somersault. Only Charles Weiffenbach, Managing Director of Delahaye, realized the danger and tried to organize an alliance between those manufacturers whom the newcomer might directly threaten, but none of them would listen to him.

It soon became obvious that Citroën knew what he was doing and that he would succeed. If the somersault did come—and that after fifteen years—it was for reasons that had nothing to do with mass production. It was also plain that if they wanted to survive, the manufacturers of cars intended for the general public would have to heed Citroën's ideas, including his methods of production:

—a complete car, with its bodywork, tyres, and equipment, at a time when a good number of luxury cars were still fitted with acetylene lighting and the electric starter was, in the true sense of the word, an accessory;

—a car that was easy to drive and look after, demanding no athletic qualities or specialized knowledge;

—an economical car, to buy, to run, and to repair, by virtue of its design and construction, but also because it would be backed up by a dealer network and after-sales service such as nobody had ever dared to imagine.

To achieve these results, it was necessary to conceive a car based on entirely fresh techniques, which could only be built by new methods, and which would be sold, serviced and repaired under a completely novel system. These three forward steps demanded similar progress in commercial organization, including the distribution of spare parts and the standardization of repair procedures.

Before Citroën, the term 'standard production car' was vaguely disparaging. Thanks to Citroën, it became synonymous with quality, because only mass production, with the enormous resources which it made available, could afford to establish such vigorous checks at every stage of manufacture and to install the latest machine tools; unless one were to enter the domain of the very costly automobiles, built one by one.

Renault and Peugeot, the leading French manufacturers in terms of production figures, adopted more or less well, more or less quickly, the aims and methods of Citroën, and they accepted mass production for their cars of moderate size. Some of the smaller manufacturers were also able to reorganize themselves, and they survived. In every case, to a greater or lesser extent, sooner or later, they followed the 'crazy' ideas of Citroën, the man who, as Louis Renault said, 'kept them from sleeping'.

Citroën: the type A open touring car

p. dumont

Right: 5th April 1919. One of the first advertisements published by Citroën, two months before deliveries began. It was the start of a new era for the motor-car, in all its branches: design, manufacture, advertising, sales, service, repairs

1919: the Citroën factory where, for the first time in Europe, cars were built on an assembly line

THE INFLUENCE OF CITROËN

After the innovation, nay revolution, caused by the introduction in 1919 of his type A, André Citroën continued to harass and perturb the other French manufacturers by going into production in 1922 with the 5 cv, the first, genuine motor-car in miniature, and also by adopting the all-steel body in 1924. This was the primary step towards the safety car and marked real progress in the construction, maintenance and repair of bodywork.

The 5 cv immediately made obsolete, and rendered useless or even ridiculous, all the economy-cars produced until then, just as, three years earlier, the type A had made its competitors seem out of date. This progress was not confined to Citroën, but reverberated among other manufacturers who strove to find new formulae; to give just one example, the 5 cv Peugeot replaced the Quadrilette.

The same evolution took place, at more or less short intervals, for other Peugeot models and, naturally, at the Renault factory, where the 6 cv and especially the 10 cv received a good number of improvements, because of Citroën. It is however only fair to add that of these three manufacturers, Citroën was the last to adopt four-wheel brakes, in October 1925 to be precise, which is just outside the period covered by this book.

The first Citroën suspension by superimposed quarter-elliptic springs, employed on types A, B2, B10, and B12

1922: the second 10 cv Citroën, or B2

Before encountering the desert sands—crossing the Sahara and on the Citroën Central African Expedition (Croisière Noire)—André Citroën's caterpillars showed their capabilities in the Alps and the Pyrenees, as well as on the dunes of Pylat, near Arcachon

December 1922/January 1923: first crossing of the Sahara. October 1924/June 1925: the Citroën caterpillars conquered Africa

A Citroën B2 with a body built by Driguet in the style of the Caddy

1924: the first all-steel Citroën, the B10 in its open touring form

*Sturdiness, ease of handling, and economy were three qualities of the
5 cv Citroën. This view emphasizes a fourth: its elegance, due to the
originality and balance of its lines*

*Right: the 5 cv Citroën is today greatly sought after by collectors: this
one has been restored and is still ready, at 55 years of age, to take the
road again*

*The 10 cv Renault, shown here with cabriolet coachwork, was the first
new post-war model, but this was scarcely evident at first glance*

The first 6 cv, the type KJ of late 1922, retained the traditional Renault bonnet but, unlike the other models of this make, it had a detachable cylinder head

In 1923, Renaults—this is a 6 cv type KJ1—received a new bonnet with sharp angles: they were to retain this until the Paris Show of 1929, when the radiator was at last mounted in front. The one exception was the Reinastella which, under its original name of Renahuit, replaced the 40 cv at the 1928 Show and always had the radiator in front

4569

*Renault, 1923: The 10 cv became KZ when it was endowed with the
new bonnet*

Renault, 1924: dynamometer testing of chassis

1924: fitting the engines to the chassis in the Renault factory at Billancourt

*1920: the Peugeot 163, rival of the 10 cv Renault and the Citroën A
and B2*

Cyclecars and Small Sports Cars

The post-war period saw the birth of a new kind of car, the cyclecar. This resulted from a legal formula which, just for once, did not crush the motorist with taxes and duties, but it did complicate the work of manufacturers by imposing a weight limit of 350 kg that they must not exceed. (The fiscal provisions defining the characteristics of a cyclecar, issued in 1919, also specified a vehicle with two seats and an engine of less than 1100 cc, for which an annual tax of 100 francs was payable.)

Except for Peugeot, only the 'new boys' threw themselves into the cyclecar adventure, and most of those who specialized in this way did not produce real cars. Nearly all of them, instead of making smaller copies of classic chassis, rushed without any proper research into designs of which originality at any price was the aim, in the sacred name of weight reduction.

In spite of the technical interest provided by a few of these machines, the cyclecar formula only managed to live from hand to mouth for a bare ten years, notwithstanding certain sporting activities. Only two manufacturers got out of the game intact, Amilcar and Salmson, which was fair because they had deviated least from traditional automobile techniques and, soon exceeding the fatal weight limit, produced many excellent little cars for more or less sporting purposes; they also made some remarkable small capacity racing cars.

Diverse other makes joined them in this category of sports cars, without first passing through the cyclecar stage.

Peugeot, having tested the cyclecar formula with the relatively conventional Quadrilette, soon moved on to the small touring car with their 5 cv. It is true that in this sphere, as in others, the influence and participation of Citroën altered many things.

ANYTHING GOES

In the cyclecar category, imagination ran riot and ideas reached white heat. Anything was allowed, it even seemed that everything was respectable, though one cannot quite see why the constructors felt obliged to build such bizarre creations when they were only asked to build light.

The Lafitte cyclecar of 1923 was fitted with an air-cooled engine, having three cylinders arranged as a star, with dimensions of 62·5 × 80 mm (748 cc). This was pivoted on the chassis, in such a way that it could be tipped forwards or backwards by the aid of a long lever. The flywheel had an egg-shaped face, with which a correspondingly contoured disc, sliding on the propeller shaft, could make full contact to give a direct drive when the engine was in the central position. By merely tilting the engine, it was possible to change the position of frictional contact between these two organs, giving an infinitely variable gear reduction; moving the flywheel into contact with the disc, on the other side of the central point, would reverse the car. The independent front suspension was on the old Lancia system, with sliding stub axles and enclosed coil springs, the rear axle being on quarter-elliptic springs. The front track was 1·10 m (3 ft

Two views of the 1922 Benjamin chassis: the manufacturers had evidently sought lightness, simplicity, and a resemblance to the Quadrilette

7·3 in), rear 1·0 m (3 ft 3·4 in), the wheelbase was 2·30 m (7 ft 0·6 in), and naturally there was no differential, which was practically the rule for cyclecars.

Fitted with a classic side-valve Ruby engine, with four cylinders of 55 × 95 mm (903 cc), later 57 × 95 mm (970 cc), and two-speed, then three-speed, gearbox, the 1924 Dalila cyclecar was distinguished by its interconnected front and rear suspension. The principle, though not the means, was to reappear much later on the 2 cv Citroën. On the Dalila, there was a long, single semi-elliptic spring mounted beside each longitudinal member of the chassis and attached thereto, centre to centre. The ends of these springs, front and rear, were coupled to the axles by shackles and pivoted levers.

The Blériot cyclecar consisted of a wooden chassis (ash without metal reinforcement), four quarter-elliptic springs, a 750 cc two-stroke engine, and a multiple disc clutch with a three-speed gearbox; it was thus relatively classic.

The Régina had only three wheels, with one in front, and it was powered by the usual 903 cc side-valve Ruby engine, mounted transversely at the rear, in unit with a three-speed gearbox. A short, articulated driveshaft transmitted the power to the left rear wheel. The Mourre cyclecar had a two-stroke engine, built under Sicam licence, and it had yet another example of friction drive. The gearchange operated by sliding a friction wheel across the face of a flat plate, which was driven by the engine, while the clutch pedal separated the two members or allowed them to resume contact; the final drive was by chain. The Carteret cyclecar was another of those with a Ruby engine and friction drive. This consisted of an assembly containing various linkages, sliding couplings and levers, and naturally the usual driving plate and friction wheel.

A choice of the four-cylinder Ruby or a two-cylinder Train engine was offered with the Fournier cyclecar, which again had friction drive. The Tholomé, type A, was yet another cyclecar with a Ruby engine and friction drive, the type B having a V-twin engine and a two-speed gearbox. The Bédélia remained faithful to transmission by belts, but in 1922, the aberrant tandem seating, with the driver at the rear, was abandoned.

The Françon cyclecar was nearer both in appearance and construction, to a real car and, radiator excepted, was not without some resemblance to the 5 cv Citroën. The family likeness ended there because its engine was a two-cylinder two-stroke of 500 cc, later 675 cc, and it too was equipped with a friction transmission. Much simpler than some of those mentioned above, it consisted in its essentials of the usual pair of plates at right angles, one of which could slide along its shaft to give an infinite number of gear reductions.

PEUGEOT AND BENJAMIN

The Quadrilette Peugeot was also in the cyclecar category, with a four-cylinder engine of 50 × 85 mm (668 cc) that had a non-detachable cylinder head. Its two original features were the chassis frame, in the shape of a platform pressed from sheet steel, and the three-speed gearbox in unit with the rear axle, which was without a differential and therefore had a very narrow track. The first version of the Quadrilette was offered in two forms, the type 161 having two seats in tandem and central steering, with a front track of 0·92 m (3 ft 0·2 in), rear 0·75 m (2 ft 5·5 in). The type 161 E (Enlarged) had staggered seats on a wider platform but the dimensions were identical. In 1922 it became type 172, better proportioned and with less scanty bodywork, which was available either with side-by-side seating or the staggered arrangement. Evolving and adding weight, it was transformed in 1924 into an elegant and comfortable 5 cv.

The Benjamin looked as if it were a replica of the Quadrilette; types A and B had a four-cylinder 4 cv engine of 54 × 82 mm (751 cc) and a three-speed gearbox combined with the back axle. In 1923, the type C Benjamin became more spacious and there was a sports model with an overhead-camshaft engine. After that, the chassis was

The curious interconnected suspension of the Dalila cyclecar of 1922/24: there was a single leaf spring on either side and a pivoted lever for each wheel

lengthened and Benjamin went over to two-stroke engines, with two and three cylinders, returning to four-strokes with an overhead-valve, four-cylinder Chapuis-Dornier power unit. The firm ceased production in 1926, having just launched a rear-engined, two-cylinder, four-stroke car.

Benjamin enjoyed a relative success commercially, for as long as the make remained faithful to its original ideas. However, the firm found the cyclecar formula too limited, and tried to free itself from its constraints without really taking up orthodox car construction—the result being disaster.

The Françon cyclecar

Left: the Fournier cyclecar

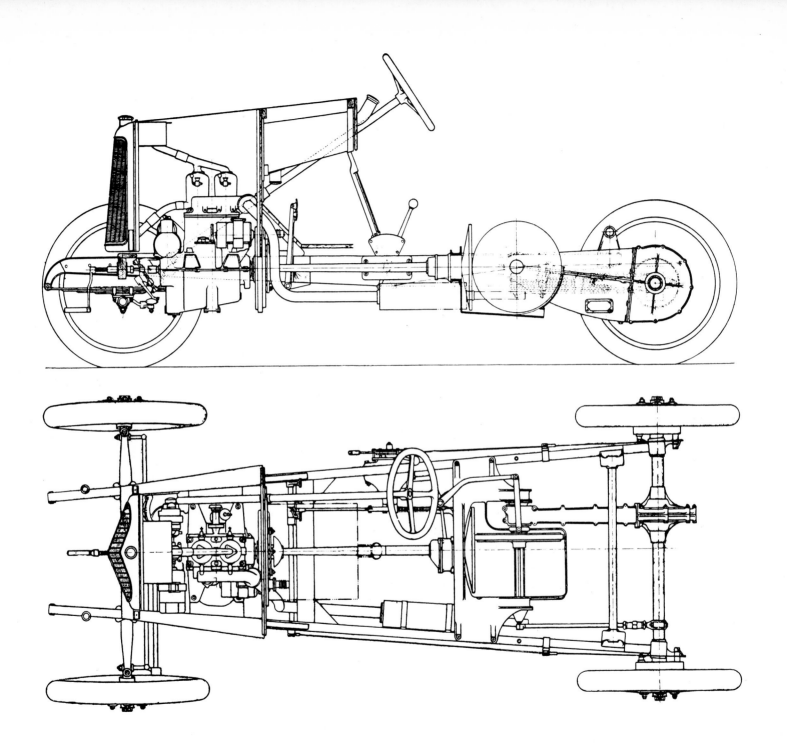

Two views of the chassis of the Françon cyclecar showing the transmission arrangements: the plate on the end of the propshaft drives the other plate that slides at right angles to it, which is connected to the rear axle by a chain

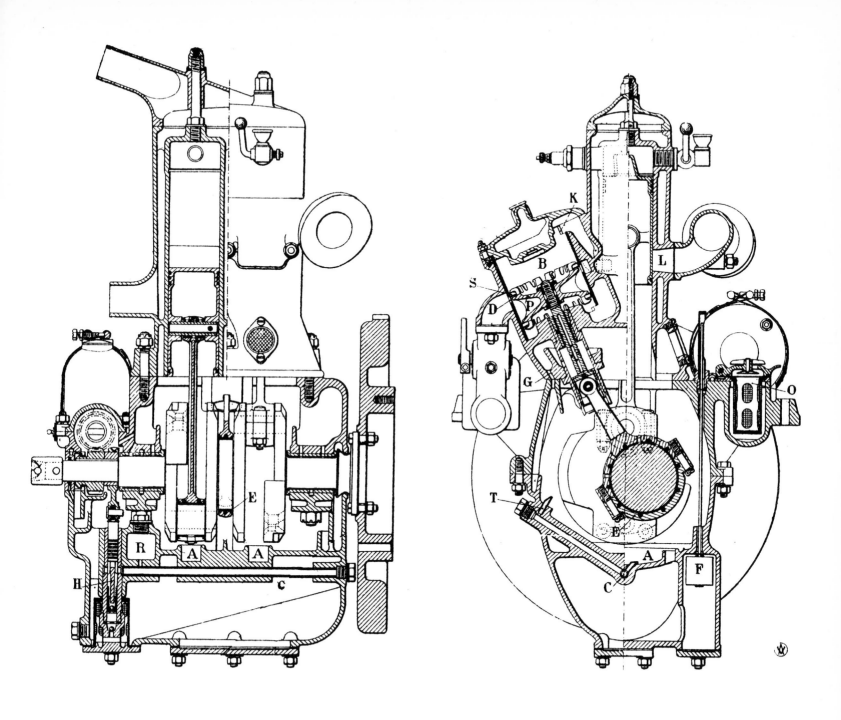

The two-stroke engine, patented by Chedru, of the Françon cyclecar

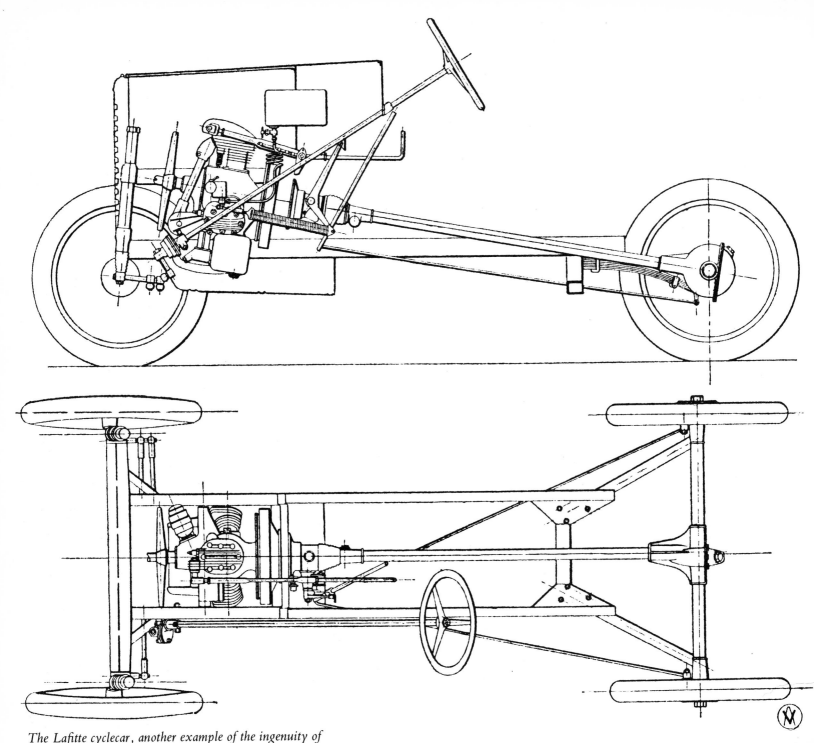

*The Lafitte cyclecar, another example of the ingenuity of
experimenters . . . and the success of conventional designs*

Tholomé: the cyclecar, even when dressed up to look like a motor-car, often had a body of ungraceful proportions

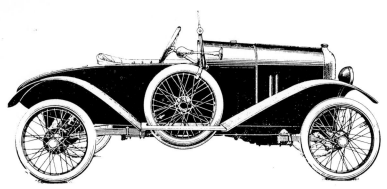

The first Amilcar, type CC

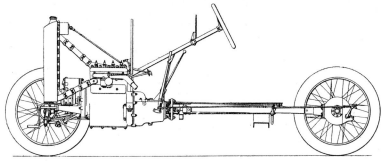

The chassis of the Amilcar CC

SOME UNUSUAL CYCLECARS

The cyclecars at which we have just been looking were intended for the working man and none of them were designed to have a high performance or to be used for sporting purposes—apart from a sports version of the Benjamin and some very special Quadrilettes. The English GN cyclecar (Godfrey and Nash), built in France under licence from 1920 by Salmson, was destined no doubt for the same utilitarian employment, though one saw them converted for racing later on.

The engine of the Salmson-GN cyclecar was an air-cooled V-twin of 84 × 98 mm (1087 cc). Once again a cyclecar could be distinguished from a motor-car by the originality of its transmission. In the case of the Salmson-GN it was composed of a somewhat complicated system of sprockets, chains and dogs, which was rather noisy but very effective.

The Darmont, a French version of the Morgan

While continuing the manufacture of the GN, type AF, for a while, Salmson launched the type AL in 1922, under the technical direction of Emile Petit. It was a cyclecar of much more classic conception, built on automobile lines, with a four-cylinder engine of 62 × 90 mm (1087 cc), the inclined valves in hemispherical combustion chambers being operated by a single rocker per cylinder. The clutch was an inverted cone, the gearbox had three speeds, and the rear axle was without a differential. The body styles were touring and sports two-seaters, a three-seater small car, a cabriolet, and a light van.

Built under licence by Salmson: the GN cyclecar

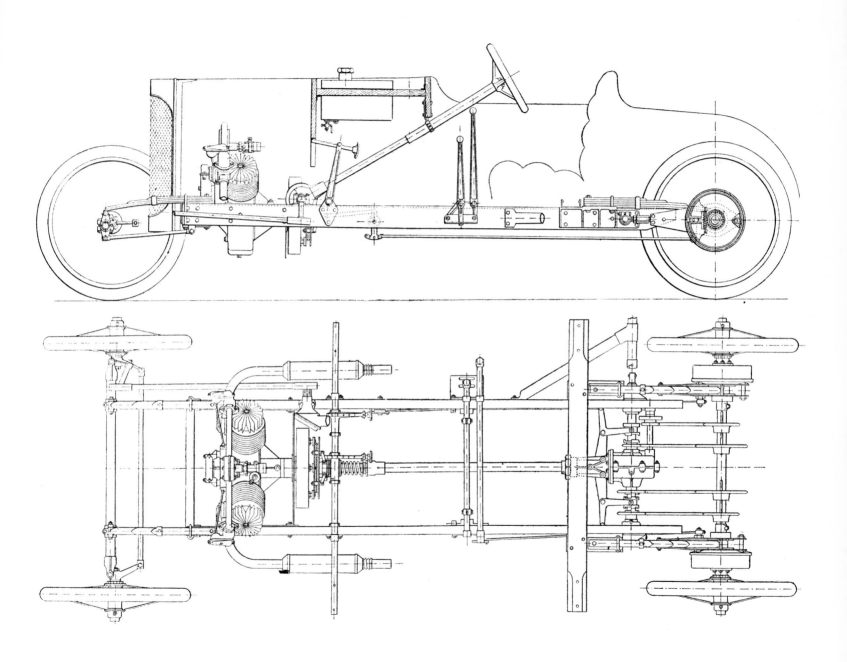

In 1923, Salmson began production of a real car of medium capacity, the 10 cv type D, four cylinders 65 × 90 mm (1195 cc), with twin overhead camshafts driven by a vertical shaft and skew gears at the front of the engine; the gearbox had three, later four, speeds. The 10 cv Salmson was the first car with twin overhead camshafts to go into series production. Also in 1923, the first Grand Sport Salmson was introduced. In essentials, it was the type AL chassis, fitted with a 10 cv engine brought within the 1100 cc class by reducing the bore to 62 mm, from which different versions were derived for nearly the next 10 years.

The great rival of the Salmson in the races was the Amilcar, as we shall see further on. Founded by Messrs. Lamy and Akkar, the Amilcar firm began production in 1921 of their type CC, a small vehicle that complied with the cyclecar regulations but which, like the Salmson AL, was a proper little motor-car. It had been designed by Moyet, a collaborator of Jules Salomon, the creator of the type A Citroën, Moyet himself being the principal designer of the 5 cv Citroën. The side-valve engine had four cylinders of 55 × 95 mm (903 cc), with a three-speed gearbox and quarter-elliptic springs all round, the track and wheelbase being 1·10 m (3 ft 7·3 in) × 2·31 m (7 ft 7 in). The only concessions to the cyclecar formula were a steel-reinforced wooden front axle beam on the first models and the absence of a differential.

The engine size rose to 57 × 95 mm (970 cc) with the type CS in 1922, then to 58 × 95 mm (1004 cc) with the type C4, which also had its wheelbase lengthened to 2·45 m (8 ft 0·5 in). Naturally, sporting versions of these models appeared and Amilcar, after entering various prototypes in competition events, commercialized the type CGS in 1924 with semi-

The first Salmson cyclecar, type AL, with four cylinders

elliptic front springs, four-wheel brakes, and an engine of 60 × 95 mm (1074 cc).

VROOM—VROOM—VROOM

The cyclecars, the real ones, remained what they had always been and disappeared, impotent in their struggle against the 5 cv Citroën. The others, those which were really little motor-cars and which could out-perform the 5 cv Citroën, survived; such were Salmson and Amilcar. They endured all the better if they evolved rapidly into exclusively sporting machines, and while the cyclecar sank into oblivion there was born, in the wake of Salmson and Amilcar, a whole generation of little cars which were more or less within the cyclecar limits of 350 kg and 1100 cc, but which had nothing in common with the hybrid devices that had been typical of the category. Examples of these were:

—the MASE, produced by *La Manufacture d' Auto- mobiles, outillage et cycles de Saint-Etienne* and designed by René Legrain-Eiffel, touring 60 × 88 mm (995 cc), sports 60 × 97 mm (1097 cc);

—the Hinstin, built by Jacques Hinstin, the man of Citroën herringbone gears and Kegresse caterpillar tracks, with a pushrod engine of 62 × 91 mm (1099 cc);

—the Mauve, created by Eugène Mauve, the father of the Bol d'Or, with an overhead-camshaft Anzani engine of 62 × 90 mm (1087 cc);

—the d'Yrsan three-wheeler, with a Ruby engine of 57 × 95 mm (970 cc), later 59 × 100 mm (1094 cc);

—the BNC, at first with a Train V-twin engine of 80 × 99 mm (995 cc), then with a four-cylinder, side-valve SCAP of 55 × 94 mm (893 cc);

—the Derby, the Rally, the Sénéchal, not forgetting the Morgan three-wheeler, of English origin, made in France under licence by Darmont.

Le Cyclecar et la Voiturette (3 places)
« SALMSON »

Type A. L. 1923

4 cylindres

Refroidissement par eau

3 vitesses marche AR

Éclairage électrique

5 roues, etc.

LE MEILLEUR MARCHÉ

à

l'achat

et à

l'usage

Le Cyclecar «SALMSON» pour le tourisme économique
SE LIVRE : En châssis nu, Torpédo tourisme, Torpédo sport

En 1921 :

VAINQUEUR DU GRAND PRIX DU MANS
CHAMPION DE FRANCE (VITESSE)

En 1922 :

GRAND PRIX DE FRANCE
GRAND PRIX DE BOULOGNE
COUPE PICKETT (2e ANNÉE)
VAINQUEUR DES 200 MILES DE BROOKLAND
etc...

SOUPLESSE
—
RAPIDITÉ

ÉCONOMIE
—
SURETÉ
DE MARCHE

La Voiturette « SALMSON » (3 places)

SALON DE L'AUTOMOBILE
ESPLANADE DES INVALIDES
STAND 47

Société des Moteurs SALMSON, 3, Avenue des Moulineaux, BILLANCOURT

Peugeot, one of the first Quadrilettes

Left: a Salmson advertisement for the 1922 Paris Show

The Peugeot Quadrilette in its second version

When fitted with this special coachwork, the Peugeot Quadrilette was developing into a real car . . .

Racing Cars

TALBOT OF SURESNES AND ELSEWHERE

In the realm of pure speed, four names head the honours list of French manufacturers: Talbot, Bugatti, Delage and Ballot.

Talbot raced mostly in the category for small cars up to 1500 cc, appearing in such events as the 200 Miles Race at Brooklands or the Coupe des Voiturettes at Le Mans. They ran two types of four-cylinder cars and the first, in 1921, had dimensions of 65 × 112 mm (1486 cc), an aluminium cylinder block with detachable steel liners, and twin overhead camshafts operating four valves per cylinder; the power output was 60 bhp at 3000 rpm and the chassis, with a track of 1·10 m (3 ft 7·3 in) and a wheelbase of 2·35 m (7 ft 8·5 in), had no differential.

The second, in 1923, had an engine of 67 × 105 mm (1481 cc) which featured a welded-up cylinder block with sheet-steel water jackets, twin overhead camshafts operating two valves per cylinder, and a ball-bearing crankshaft. It developed 70 bhp at 5000 rpm and was capable of 170 km/h (106 mph); the track was 1·18 m (3 ft 10·4 in), wheelbase 2·18 m (7 ft 1·8 in), and again there was no differential. Fitted with a Roots supercharger in 1924, the speed rose to 190 km/h (118 mph) on a power output of 100 bhp at 5250 rpm. This second Talbot—if not the first too—was the work of the elderly Bertarione, formerly of Fiat, and his assistant Becchia. Bertarione then left for a short spell with Hotchkiss, but returned later to Talbot to work again with Walter Becchia. Long afterwards, Becchia worked for Citroën on the engines for the 2 cv and the DS 19.

Another Talbot took part in the Grand Prix of the Automobile Club de France at Le Mans in 1921. This was a three-litre straight eight of 65 × 112 mm (2972 cc), designed in England by the Frenchman, Louis Coatalen, and which ran at different times under the names of the three makes that formed the STD combine, Sunbeam, Talbot, and Darracq. It had an aluminium cylinder block with liners, twin overhead camshafts and four valves per cylinder, and it developed 108 bhp at 4000 rpm. The best-placed Talbot, that of Boillot, finished fifth in the Grand Prix, but another, this time with a Sunbeam radiator, won the 1922 Tourist Trophy.

ETTORE BUGATTI'S THOROUGHBREDS

Bugatti excelled particularly in races for small cars during the 1920–25 period such as the Coupe des Voiturettes at Le Mans in 1920 and the Grand Prix of Italy at Brescia in 1921, thanks to his little 16-valve models. His first eight-cylinder racing cars always contested the lead but then often suffered from bad luck. In the 1922 GP at Strasbourg, a Bugatti finished second after Friderich led for most of the race and then retired. There was the defeat at Monza through tyre troubles, the retirement of four out of five cars with lubrication problems at the 1923 Indianapolis 500, and a third place in the GP at Tours, after the other two team members had crashed through bad roadholding.

In 1924, at the GP of the ACF run on the Lyons circuit, Bugatti put on the starting grid five examples of a new racing

1921: the first 1500 cc Talbot

The five-litre hillclimb Delage, restored and cherished by an English collector, Nigel Arnold-Forster

The two-litre Delage as raced in the 1924 French Grand Prix at Lyons

car that caused a sensation, the type 35. Once again, tyre problems brought about the defeat of Bugatti and only two cars finished, in seventh and eighth places. The type 35 redeemed itself by racing hard every Sunday for seven or eight years on all the circuits. It is true that, built as a production car and sold relatively cheaply to a great number of drivers, the type 35 had by far the greatest number of entries in Grand Prix races, as well as in the less important events where the opposition was negligible.

The Bugatti type 35 owed its successes to its road-going qualities—handling, ease of driving, roadholding—rather than to its power and maximum speed, which were inferior to those of its rivals. Designed by an artist, it was, down to the smallest detail, of an extraordinary beauty.

THE METEORS OF LOUIS DELAGE

Three Delages were particularly prominent during this epoch:

—a five-litre car built in 1922, intended especially for hillclimbs, with a six-cylinder pushrod engine of 85 × 150 mm (5107 cc), developing 170 bhp at 3600 rpm;

—la Torpille (the Torpedo), a car built in 1924 to take speed records on the road, a V12 with pushrods operated by a single camshaft, 90 × 140 mm (10688 cc), developing 280 bhp at 3000 rpm, which covered the flying kilometre at Arpajon at 230·585 km/h (143·273 mph);

—a two-litre 12-cylinder car which, after a disastrous first appearance, can be considered as the best French racing car of the era, because of the successes gained in its second, and particularly its third, seasons.

Designed by Planchon and Lory, the two-litre Delage, as run in the GP at Tours in 1923, had 12 cylinders arranged in a 60° V of 51·3 × 80 mm (1984 cc), with twin overhead camshafts for each bank of cylinders and a crankshaft on seven roller bearings; the track and wheelbase were 1·25 m

A 16-valve Bugatti before the Coupe des Voiturettes at Le Mans in 1920

184

(4 ft 1·2 in) × 2·60 m (8 ft 6·2 in) and the weight was 660 kg (1452 lbs). With 116 bhp at 8000 rpm, the 12-cylinder Delage was capable of 180 km/h (112 mph), but it suffered from cooling problems.

Driven at Tours by René Thomas, the car retired, and when it reappeared at the GP of the ACF in 1924 at Lyons, it had a slightly modified chassis with a front track of 1·30 m (4 ft 3·2 in), rear 1·20 m (3 ft 11·2 in), and a new body with a radiator more closely resembling those of the production models. Above all an entirely new oiling system, to cure the overheating, employed three pumps: one for the crankshaft bearings, another for the camshafts, and a third to scavenge the sump, passing the lubricant to a combined radiator and tank which fed the other two pumps. Divo finished second and the other two Delages were third and sixth.

The Grand Prix of the ACF took place at Montlhéry on 26th July 1925, to inaugurate the new 'Autodrome', and the 12-cylinder Delages were first and second in the hands of Benoist/Divo and Wagner/Torchy. Fitted with two Roots superchargers, they developed 205 bhp at 6500 rpm and attained 215 km/h (133·6 mph).

EDOUARD BALLOT—AN UNLUCKY MAN

The story goes that it was only on Christmas Eve, 1918, that Edouard Ballot decided to build some cars for the 500 miles race at Indianapolis. True or false, four Ballots, designed by Ernest Henry who had already been responsible for the brilliant pre-war, twin-cam Peugeots, were embarked at Le Havre four months later, 26th April 1919. Faster than their rivals during practice, they suffered the consequences of badly chosen axle ratios and a hurried change of wheel sizes, the first of the Ballots finishing fourth. The engines were straight eights of 74 × 140 mm (4817 cc) with twin overhead camshafts, developing 140 bhp at 3000 rpm.

In 1920, Ballot again entered for the 500 miles race at Indianapolis with some more eight-cylinder, twin-cam cars of 65 × 112 mm (2973 cc), which developed 108 bhp at

A Bugatti for the Grand Prix of Strasbourg in 1922. The exhaust was discharged through the pointed tail

Indianapolis 1923 : a Bugatti single-seater

. . . and after

Ettore Bugatti's masterpiece: the type 35. Let no-one speak, even today, of styling or design . . .

3800 rpm. Although they were the fastest, they only finished second, fifth, and seventh, and bad luck pursued the Ballot team throughout the 1921 season. One of the cars led the GP of the ACF for seven laps and was eliminated by a stone through the petrol tank, and misfortune continued in 1923 at the Targa Florio and Indianapolis.

SOME OTHER RACERS

Peugeot returned to Grand Prix racing after the war, without any great success, with new cars which owed nothing to Ernest Henry. In 1923, Rolland Pilain presented an interesting straight eight of 59 × 90 mm (1968 cc), with twin overhead camshafts and four carburettors. It won the GP of San Sebastian and took part in the GP of Tours.

Some manufacturers, unexpected in this sphere, took part in competition work. Mathis, for instance, raced a four-cylinder car of 58 × 100 mm (1057 cc) in 1920 and entered another one of 69 × 100 mm (1496 cc) in the GP of the ACF; La Licorne also raced, of which we have previously spoken.

Even the Model T Ford appeared in racing trim, radically altered by Montier, a French tuner. In the 1500 cc class, alongside the Amilcars, Salmsons, and Derbys, some pretty little cars raced under the evocative name of La Perle. This make made its first appearance in the Grand Prix des Voiturettes at Le Mans in 1921, with three cars consisting of Malicet et Blin chassis fitted with Bignan engines of 1400 cc; these had two camshafts in the crank case, operating side-valves under T-heads. From these engines, Némorin Causan developed an overhead-valve version in 1922, of 63 × 119 mm (1491 cc), and in 1924 he designed a new six-cylinder unit of 60 × 88 mm (1493 cc), with a single overhead camshaft. Though the La Perle was intended as a touring rather than a sports car, it was often entered in competition events, both by the works and by private owners. The four-cylinder models raced at Boulogne and at hillclimbs, notably Gaillon, and also took part in the records day at Arpajon, while the six-cylinder car recorded a time of 35·6 seconds for the standing kilometre, at the end of its career in 1928.

Bugatti, the straight-eight engine of the type 35

A Very Special Car

We have just made a trip—express—round the manufacturers of French cars from 1920 to 1925. We have seen cyclecars and limousines of great luxury, mass production chassis—and if we have uncovered some original designs, all the vehicles that we have reviewed had at least one point in common: they were propelled by one or two wheels. Here, to finish, is a car that is an exception to that rule, the propeller-driven Leyat, whose production in the early twenties was limited to just a few examples. One of them completed the run from Paris to Bordeaux in 12 hours, in 1921.

The Leyat